CAN LABOUR WIN?

About Policy Network

Policy Network is an international thinktank and research institute. Its network spans national borders across Europe and the wider world with the aim of promoting the best progressive thinking on the major social and economic challenges of the 21st century.

Our work is driven by a network of politicians, policymakers, business leaders, public service professionals, and academic researchers who work on long-term issues relating to public policy, political economy, social attitudes, governance and international affairs. This is complemented by the expertise and research excellence of Policy Network's international team.

A platform for research and ideas

• Promoting expert ideas and political analysis on the key economic, social and political challenges of our age.
• Disseminating research excellence and relevant knowledge to a wider public audience through interactive policy networks, including interdisciplinary and scholarly collaboration.
• Engaging and informing the public debate about the future of European and global progressive politics.

A network of leaders, policymakers and thinkers

• Building international policy communities comprising individuals and affiliate institutions.
• Providing meeting platforms where the politically active, and potential leaders of the future, can engage with each other across national borders and with the best thinkers who are sympathetic to their broad aims.
• Engaging in external collaboration with partners including higher education institutions, the private sector, thinktanks, charities, community organisations, and trade unions.
• Delivering an innovative events programme combining in-house seminars with large-scale public conferences designed to influence and contribute to key public debates.

www.policy-network.net

CAN LABOUR WIN?

The Hard Road to Power

Patrick Diamond and Giles Radice with Penny Bochum

policy network

ROWMAN &
LITTLEFIELD
INTERNATIONAL

London • New York

Published by Rowman & Littlefield International Ltd.
Unit A, Whitacre, 26-34 Stannary Street, London, SE11 4AB
www.rowmaninternational.com

Rowman & Littlefield International Ltd. is an affiliate of Rowman & Littlefield
4501 Forbes Boulevard, Suite 200, Lanham, Maryland 20706, USA
With additional offices in Boulder, New York, Toronto (Canada), and Plymouth (UK)
www.rowman.com

British Library Cataloguing in Publication Data
A catalogue record for this book is available from the British Library

ISBN: PB 978-1-78348-544-4

Library of Congress Cataloging-in-Publication Data
Library of Congress Control Number: 2015949970

♾ ™ The paper used in this publication meets the minimum requirements
of American National Standard for Information Sciences—Permanence of Paper
for Printed Library Materials, ANSI/NISO Z39.48-1992.

Printed in the United States of America

CONTENTS

ABOUT THE AUTHORS

Patrick Diamond is vice-chair of Policy Network. He is a lecturer in Public Policy at Queen Mary, University of London, Gwilym Gibbon fellow at Nuffield College, Oxford, and a visiting fellow in the Department of Politics at the University of Oxford. Until May 2010 he was head of policy planning in 10 Downing Street and senior policy adviser to the prime minister.

Giles Radice is a Labour member of the House of Lords. He was formerly the member of parliament for Durham North and was chairman of the treasury select committee from 1997–2001. He is the author of numerous successful political and historical titles.

Patrick and Giles co-authored Policy Network's 2010 pamphlet *Southern Discomfort Again*, which served as a sequel to the original *Southern Discomfort* series published after Labour's 1992 general election defeat.

ACKNOWLEDGEMENTS

The authors would like to thank Policy Network, especially Michael McTernan, Alastair Reed, Robert Philpot, Ben Dilks and Roger Liddle, and their excellent team for supporting this project. We would like in particular to thank Penny Bochum for her brilliant research work in analysing the election results, interviewing party activists, carrying out telephone interviews, and support throughout the preparation of this publication. We would also like to thank Bobby Duffy, Gideon Skinner and Glenn Gottfried at Ipsos Mori for their quantitative research.

EXECUTIVE SUMMARY

After its disastrous defeat in 2015, Labour is at grave risk of throwing away the 2020 general election. The party has to understand why it suffered such a devastating defeat on 7 May and learn crucial lessons if it is to recover. The reasons appear obvious enough: the British public did not believe that Ed Miliband was a credible prime minister; they feared that a Labour government would plunge the British economy back into chaos; and they perceived that the party was out of touch on issues like immigration and welfare. Labour was not just narrowly defeated in 2015, it was overwhelmingly rejected by an electorate who no longer trust or respect the party. Underlying all of this is a sense that Labour is a party that does not understand the modern world, wedded to an outdated 'cloth cap' image of heavy industry and the impersonal bureaucracy of the public sector. The risk for the Labour party, like social democratic parties across Europe, is further electoral defeat and, then inevitably, permanent irrelevance.

As of today, there are few signs that the party grasps why it lost and, in particular, why swing voters in marginal seats were not prepared to vote Labour. A party that does not understand why it was defeated scarcely deserves to be taken seriously by the electorate. This publication examines why Labour lost the trust of voters so overwhelmingly, and, crucially, how the party under a new leader can win them back by 2020 – charting Labour's hard road back to power.

INTRODUCTION

Why Did Labour Lose?

There is no escaping this chilling fact: the Labour party suffered a crushing defeat at the May 2015 general election, finishing nearly 100 seats behind the Conservatives. This was one of the worst results in our history. Understandably, this beating has shocked and dismayed many Labour supporters. But we say that the party should not despair. Labour can win. However, to achieve victory in 2020, we have to recognise both the scale and nature of our defeat, accept that the world has changed and launch a major revision of our ideas, strategy and policies.[1]

Labour ought to have been able to do better in May. After all, the coalition parties were unpopular having overseen a long recession and a fragile recovery, accompanied by declining living standards which only in 2015 began to pick up. Above all, the major governing party, the Conservatives, was seen as socially exclusive and out of touch with modern Britain. Yet, despite the prediction of the opinion polls, David Cameron was able to secure an overall Conservative majority for the first time since the 1992 election.

Labour was defeated on 7 May because voters did not see it as providing a credible alternative government. The party lost because it did not have a leader whom the public regarded as a plausible prime minister. Not only did it fail to win back its reputation for

economic competence following the 2008 financial crash, but
Labour went backwards after 2010. It was all too easy for the Tories
to brand Labour as being unfit for office, because the party did not
appear to have a convincing answer on the deficit which the majority
of voters took to be the central test of economic competence. Most
of all, Labour failed to offer an optimistic and forward-looking
vision of the future which could appeal across the nation. Labour is
today too often seen as an antiquated, class-based party rooted in the
past: like so many social democratic parties across the EU, Labour
is perceived as out of touch with the modern age. As its electoral
coalition has fragmented, the party's identity is increasingly past its
sell-by date.

The Labour party's electoral strategy was glaringly inadequate
because it was apparently based on cobbling together a flimsy electoral grouping consisting of 2010 Labour voters and disgruntled
former Liberal Democrats. This took for granted that those who
voted Labour in 2010 represented an unshakeable bedrock of support and that those who backed the experienced leadership team of
Gordon Brown and Alistair Darling then would stick with Labour
under Miliband. Moreover, the disintegration of the Liberal Democrats ended up overwhelmingly benefiting the Conservatives rather
than Labour. The party had a potentially historic opportunity to heal
the breach on the centre left of British politics after the formation
of the 2010 coalition government, but it was thrown away. Labour's
strategy was too tribal and based on a caricature of 'leftwing'
Liberal Democrat voters used to justify a departure from the centre
ground. The party unwisely abandoned the approach of constructing
a broad-based electoral alliance appealing to all classes and social
constituencies which had enabled it to win three consecutive victories, in favour of a limited electoral strategy based on 35 per cent of
the electorate. Instead of seeking converts from 2010 Conservative
voters, many of whom voted Labour in 1997, 2001, and 2005, the
party focused on its so-called 'core support'. The candidates in our
survey reported that they were told to concentrate on maximising
turnout: there was no strategy to convert 'undecided' voters into

Labour 'switchers'. When Labour similarly tried to appeal to such a narrow constituency in the 1950s and the 1980s, it was, unsurprisingly, consigned to the electoral wilderness.

Those who now believe that Labour will be back in power in 2020 as the result of 'one more heave' or a dramatic swing in the electoral pendulum are naive at best, irresponsible at worst. Labour has no divine right to be a party of government. In Scotland, Labour chose to ignore the warnings of the 2007 and 2011 parliamentary elections; as a result, it now faces an existential threat. If Labour cannot compete effectively for office and provide a credible alternative to the Conservatives in the fragmented political system which now exists in Great Britain, it will be replaced by another party that can. There are those who await a financial crash and collapse in the capitalist system to provide Labour's path back to power, but their position is, as ever, tenuous at best. This is tantamount to an admission that Labour can never win under conditions of mass prosperity, and that it can only return to power by mobilising the ranks of the dispossessed and the mass unemployed. That is hardly a convincing or edifying position for a modern progressive party. The historical evidence suggests the reverse: the more severe the country's economic problems, the more likely it is that the electorate will cling on to the Conservatives, as happened in Britain throughout the 1930s.

The predicament now facing the Labour party is serious. The dire 2015 election results are summarised at the end of this chapter. The party has not won an overall parliamentary majority or indeed a major election anywhere in Britain for more than a decade. Labour's unpopularity in the Midlands and southern England outside London still cripples its chances of returning to government: in 2015 in the south-east, the south-west and the eastern regions, Labour won only 12 out of 197 seats. In the south and the Midlands as a whole, Labour holds only 51 out of 302 seats. The electoral alliance of traditional Labour supporters and middle-class voters in southern England and the Midlands has unravelled spectacularly, to the point where some doubt whether it can be reconstructed. If anything, Labour had a huge advantage in 2015 which will not be there next time: the electoral decimation of the Liberal Democrats meant the party's majorities in the north of England, where the Liberals were once strong contenders, are now exaggerated. This 'bonus' of votes from disaffected Liberal Democrat supporters will not be repeated in 2020. No one should doubt the scale of the disaster inflicted on Labour over the last five years, leaving it with an electoral mountain to climb if it is to return to government anytime in the next decade.

SOUTHERN DISCOMFORT SINCE 1992

The original work on 'southern discomfort' set out how Labour needed to change radically if it was to recover from the devastating 1992 election defeat by winning crucial seats in southern England. Labour's 'southern problem' was not primarily geographical: it was the product of social change as underlying shifts in political attitudes made Labour's language and appeal less and less relevant to people's lives. Under Tony Blair and Gordon Brown, Labour responded to the challenge by broadening its electoral appeal and showing that it understood the hopes and aspirations of affluent working-class and middle-class Britain. In 1997 and 2001, Labour secured landslide victories by bringing together northern England and its Celtic 'heartlands' with the Midlands and the south, an unbeatable alliance of professional workers, skilled working-class, white-collar and blue-collar voters. Labour won again in 2005 by holding on to many of these southern and Midlands' marginal seats, albeit often with wafer-thin majorities. In our pamphlet, *Southern Discomfort Again*, published after the 2010 election defeat, we warned that the party urgently needed to address its disabling weakness in southern England, a warning which was unfortunately not heeded. Marginal seats in the south that Labour has always won when it has been in government – in 1945, 1964, 1974, and 1997 – including the string of marginals in the Medway towns and north Kent – were simply written off.

Because it has few MPs left in the south, Labour is once again in danger of ignoring southern England outside London. Unquestionably, these regions are some of the richest in western Europe: they have seen the largest recovery in income per head since the financial crash; the south-east is the most productive region in the UK apart from London; and it has the highest employment rate. The Midlands is quickly catching up with London and the south-east having the highest number of 'innovation active' businesses, while incomes per head are rising. The truth is that Labour cannot win without gaining a substantial number of seats in the south and the increasingly prosperous Midlands.

It is still an extraordinary fact that after the 2015 election, Labour holds no parliamentary seats at all in large English counties such as Kent, Essex, Hertfordshire and Buckinghamshire. There are some who argue these constituencies are a distraction, and that Labour should concentrate on winning back its northern, Welsh and Scottish 'heartlands'. This is the wrong approach for three reasons. First, there are not enough seats in the north of England, Scotland and Wales for Labour to secure an overall parliamentary majority next time. Second, the rest of Britain is becoming more like the south of England and the Midlands in terms of its standard of living, demographic characteristics and social attitudes. If Labour cannot win in the south, increasingly it will not be able to win anywhere in Britain. Third, Labour must aspire to be a national party representing voters across the four constituent nations of the UK and from all sections of society, just as it did in 1945, 1964 and 1997. Clement Attlee's victory after the second world war was achieved by making spectacular gains in once impregnable Conservative strongholds: outer London, East Anglia, and a slew of towns across southern England.

With every election defeat, attention inevitably turns to the question of Labour's support among working-class voters. The accusation is that, under New Labour, the party 'lost five million voters' between 1997 and 2010, particularly in social group DE who traditionally formed the bedrock of Labour's support, with 'core' voters becoming disaffected following the rightwards shift in the Blair government's policies on the economy, welfare, immigration, civil liberties and, of course, Iraq. It is said that only if it reverses that tide can Labour win again. However, Miliband attempted to do so in 2015 by running on the most conventionally 'leftwing' Labour programme since 1987. The strategy failed: Labour's support in the DE social group rose by just one per cent in comparison to the party's dismal result in 2010. Labour made up slightly more ground among the C2 voters but, among the C1 skilled working-class and white-collar workers (including many public sector professionals such as teachers and nurses), its performance was similarly unimpressive.

In any case, the proportion of people in Britain who are working class has been steadily declining. According to a recent study, the numbers employed in traditional manual working-class occupations has continued to fall as a proportion of the UK population: the researchers argue that: "The traditional working class is fading from contemporary importance."[2] The National Centre for Social Research found in 2007 that nearly 60 per cent of the British public subjectively viewed themselves as 'working class', but more recent data shows the relative decline of the working class and the relative increase in middle class occupations over the last 40 years, as illustrated in Table 1.1. British society has become more socially fluid. More than five decades ago in 1960, Anthony Crosland argued that Labour's "unique identification" with the working class, "is a clear political liability for the simple reason that the working class is shrinking in size".[3] He identified "a growing group of socially ambivalent, fluid, cross-pressured voters" who were changing the nature of the British electorate.

Table 1.1   Social class of chief income earner in UK households

	AB	C1	C2DE
1968	12	22	65
1978	16	22	62
1988	18	23	59
1998 ·	21	28	52
2008	27	29	45

Source: National Readership Survey

Labour's obsession with continuing to identify itself as an exclusively working-class party is self-defeating. It reflects a tribal culture of 'us and them' politics which, for many years, has been off-putting to centrist, middle-income, middle of the road voters whose support is needed if the party is to win elections. Under Miliband, Labour allowed its electoral base to shrink even further. In 2015, according to Ipsos Mori: "Labour only had a clear lead over the Conservatives among 18-34s, voters in social class DE, among private and social renters, and BME voters."[4] The party's support fell dramatically among those over 65, the group most likely to turn out and vote. Even among Black Minority Ethnic (BME) voters, the gap between Labour and the Conservatives is now believed to be "shrinking dramatically".[5]

The reality is that the assumptions which are made about the political priorities for working-class voters by those who claim that the Blair governments 'lost five million voters' after 1997 are more often than not inaccurate: rather than demanding a shift to the traditional left on economic and welfare issues, these voters want a governing party that defends their borders, ensures people play by the rules in what they claim from the state and is prepared to stand up for British (and English) political interests. The blue-collar skilled working class is exceptionally diverse with important differences in economic preferences on tax and redistribution, and wide variation in cultural attitudes; as Evans and Mellon point out: "21 per cent of respondents in the British Election Study (BES) who are classified as skilled manual workers in social grade are actually self-employed, the highest proportion among any of the social grade categories."[6] Like the middle classes skilled manual workers have higher expectations too: they want a better standard of living, outstandingly good public services and more opportunities for themselves and their families. They want their children to be able to own a home, have a professional career and enjoy a higher standard of life than their parents. Labour has to get to grips with the changing politics of class, or it will make itself irrelevant.

Our research reveals that voters rejected Labour in 2015 not only because it was seen to be economically incompetent and weak on leadership. Labour was also struggling in three areas where it has traditionally been strong – on fairness, on public services and on standing up for Britain. Despite Miliband's conventional pitch to the left on economic issues and his explicit criticism of business and private enterprise, there is little evidence that voters liked what they heard.

On fairness, voters believe Labour is no more likely to achieve equality and social mobility than the Conservative party – a shocking indictment given the Tories' track record in standing up for elite interests. Too many voters believe that Labour's notion of 'fairness' is about giving benefits and entitlements to those who do not really deserve them, or who abuse the system. This is not just about so-called 'benefit cheats': in the wake of the 2008 crash, voters are as resentful about 'greedy bankers' whose reckless behaviour required bailouts from hard-working taxpayers. In 2015, Labour put the battle against economic inequality at the front and centre of its programme: unfortunately, many wavering voters who do not currently earn high incomes fear that addressing inequality through higher taxes means capping their own aspirations to get on and do well.

On public services, too many voters fear that Labour will waste money and give in to producer interests. It is a tragedy that Labour, the party that built the welfare state and institutions such as the National Health Service during the post-1945 Attlee governments, is no longer trusted to manage public services efficiently. In government, Labour learned that it is not enough just to pour more money into the public sector: the state has to become more efficient and services have to be genuinely attentive to people's needs. Too many voters believed that the Labour governments between 1997 and 2010 wasted money and did not improve services speedily enough. Given their own squeezed household budgets, these voters are understand-ably resentful of government profligacy and waste. Moreover, if voters fear that Labour is likely to mess up the economy, they will never trust it to run English, Welsh or Scottish public services: it is a truism that long-term investment in health and education requires sustained economic growth.

Sadly, too many voters no longer perceive Labour to be a patriotic party as it was under Attlee and Ernest Bevin in the 1940s, Harold Wilson and James Callaghan in the 1960s and 1970s, and, yes, under Blair and Brown as well. This is despite the complicity of the previous Conservative-led government in winding down Britain's defence capabilities, and reducing the UK's influence in the world. In the 1980s, Labour lost because it was perceived to be weak on defence; in the 2010s, Labour is losing because it is perceived to be weak in standing up for national interests. The politics of national grievance have grown more visceral following the Scottish independence referendum; English voters in particular no longer believe that Labour will speak up for their political concerns. The English see Labour as embarrassed by national symbols such as the St George's flag, and too dependent on Welsh and Scottish political interests.

Next time around, the Labour party will be fighting to win on three fronts: winning English marginal seats from the Conservatives; defending its northern strongholds against the insurgent UK Independence party; and rebuilding Labour's political base in Scotland which has been completely shattered. We believe the party should be capable of advance on all these fronts. But Labour can only secure a parliamentary majority in 2020 if it is able to beat the Conservatives in English marginal seats. Labour can win back lost ground in Scotland and repel the Ukip insurgency in northern England, but it will regain office only when it is competitive against the Tories in middle England. Some Labour politicians believe the party's challenge is to win back working-class votes lost to Ukip, whereas, in fact, most of the votes Labour needs to win will be from those who voted Conservative in 2010. As the Fabian Society put it in a recent report: "Around four out of five of the extra (net) votes Labour will need to gain in English and Welsh marginals will have to come direct from Conservative voters."[7] It is on that overriding objective of winning back former Tory voters in English marginals that this publication will focus: our argument is that if Labour presents to the country economically responsible policies which appeal to people's sense of fairness as well as their self-interest, the party can win again in every part of Great Britain.

Labour will need to achieve a swing of 8.75 per cent across Britain to win outright five years from now, and that is without taking into account the full effect of further boundary changes. It can only do so by presenting a compelling vision to the country, not through narrow tactical calculation and 'micro-targeting' of electoral groups. The electorate has not shifted irrevocably to the right in its' social attitudes over the last 10 years. There are major concerns about the condition of our economy, the irresponsible practices of banks and large corporations and the future viability of our public services and welfare state. Voters across Britain still want to live in a country where we give a hand-up to those who want to get on, as well as a helping hand to those in trouble. But Labour has to offer a meaningful and plausible alternative anchored in economically credible policies, rather than the futile politics of protest and opposition.

In 2020, it will be 23 years since Labour's historic 1997 victory. The world has changed profoundly in that period: New Labour was forged against the backdrop of economic recovery and rising prosperity. Blair and Brown's mission was to distribute the gains of economic growth more fairly, while investing in public services which voters felt had been badly neglected under Margaret Thatcher and John Major. Since that time, the British model of the market economy has been gravely undermined by the financial crisis and voters have experienced rising insecurity and a squeeze on their living standards. Britain's society and economy have changed at an unprecedented rate, given rapid immigration and increasing diversity. This has brought enormous benefits, but often with too little effort to protect the most vulnerable communities. Another disturbing development has been the depth of disengagement from politicians and politics more generally. Too few voters feel that any government, Labour or Conservative, will make much difference to their lives. This is especially damaging to Labour which only succeeds when it can generate a sense of hope and optimism about the future as it did in 1945, 1964 and 1997. Labour has to do more to reconnect people with politics by tackling the corrosive decline of trust. For all of these reasons, if it is to win again Labour cannot return to the political strategy and campaign playbook of the 1990s. Our belief is that for Labour to win elections it has to listen carefully to the views of voters. This does not mean basing policy merely on what opinion polls and focus groups say: it does mean trying to understand the mood of the electorate and the changing shape of Britain in order to find a path back to power. Winning across the country is not just an act of expediency, designed to keep Labour in office irrespective of whether it can achieve its ethical mission. By securing support across the country and developing its roots in every social and geographical constituency, Labour will be better able to carry out its reforms. The radical centre-left governments of 1945, 1964 and 1997 were broad-based progressive coalitions able to unite a broad sweep of constituencies and classes.

Our research includes interviews with former parliamentary candidates, key campaign staff, and party members in marginal seats across England, Wales and Scotland. We also commissioned qualitative research with wavering voters backed up by separate telephone interviews, alongside a major quantitative survey, carried out by the polling organisation Ipsos Mori. We have sought to draw lessons from marginal seats, but our conclusions are relevant to Labour across Britain. By taking into account the needs and views of the electorate, Labour can overcome the electoral mountain it has to climb to win in 2020 – and become, once again, Britain's governing party.

THE 2015 ELECTION RESULT

Labour's target list for the 2015 election contained 106 constituencies, 86 of which were held by the Conservatives. It needed a net gain of 27 to become the largest single party and a net gain of 67 to win an overall majority. Had it taken all the target seats, it would have had a majority of 83. The target seats were in all regions of

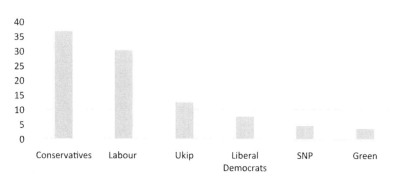

Figure 1.1   Percentage share of vote in 2015. *Source*: Data drawn from House of Commons Library Briefing Paper General Election 2015. Contains parliamentary information licensed under the Open Parliament Licence v3.0

Figure 1.2   Percentage change in vote from 2010 to 2015 election. *Source*: Data drawn from House of Commons Library Briefing Paper General Election 2015. Contains parliamentary information licensed under the Open Parliament Licence v3.0

Great Britain, although there were very few in Scotland. Thirty-one were in the south, 23 in the Midlands, and 27 in the north. In the end, Labour not only failed to take most of the target seats, but it also lost seats. Despite a small increase in vote share (+1.5 per cent), the party has 26 seats fewer than in 2010. Labour won 12 seats from the Liberal Democrats and 10 from the Conservatives; and then lost 48 seats (eight to the Conservatives and 40 to the Scottish National

Table 1.2 The UK election result in 2015

	Seats won	Change	Votes (000s)	% vote	% change
Con	330	+24	11,299.1	36.8	+0.8
Lab	232	−26	9,347.0	30.4	+1.5
SNP	56	+50	1,454.4	4.7	+3.1
Lib Dem	8	−49	2,416.0	7.9	−15.2
Plaid Cymru	3	0	181.7	0.6	0
Ukip	1	+1	3,881.1	12.6	+9.5
Green	1	0	1,157.6	3.8	+2.8
Others	19	0	959.9	3.1	−2.5

Source: Data drawn from House of Commons Library Briefing Paper General Election 2015. Contains parliamentary information licensed under the Open Parliament Licence v3.0.

party). The party failed to achieve the swing it needed in many demographic groups, or to profit significantly from the spectacular collapse of the Liberal Democrat vote; it lost voters in significant numbers to every other major party, and haemorrhaged votes among the group with the highest turnout: the over-65s. Labour lost seats or failed to make net gains in the key regions of the south-east, the south-west and the East Midlands; it made tiny gains in the West Midlands, the eastern region, Yorkshire, the north-east and north-west; and was annihilated in Scotland. Labour did better in London, but its support base was not broad enough to win bellwether marginal seats like Battersea, Hendon, Croydon Central and Harrow East. Ipsos Mori's analysis suggests that: "Among those who voted, Labour held on to 72 per cent of those who said they voted for the party in 2010."[8] Turnout in 2015 was 66.2 per cent, a slight rise compared to 65.1 per cent in 2010.

NOTES

1. This book takes its title from Anthony Crosland's seminal pamphlet, *Can Labour Win?,* launched after Labour had suffered three consecutive election defeats during the 1950s.
2. *A New Model of Social Class? Findings from the BBC's Great British Class Survey Experiment* http://soc.sagepub.com/content/47/2/219.full

3. Crosland, A. (1960), *Must Labour Lose?*, London: The Fabian Society, p. 10.

4. Ipsos Mori, 'How Britain Voted in 2015: The 2015 Election – Who Voted for Whom?', Ipsos Mori, 22 May 2015, https://www.ipsos-mori.com/researchpublications/researcharchive/3575/How-Britain-voted-in-2015.

5. Ford, R., Janta-Lipinski, L. and Sobolewska, M. 'Where Did the Million New Conservative BME Voters Go?', YouGov, 12 June 2015, https://yougov.co.uk/news/2015/06/12/are-conservatives-really-breaking-through-ethnic-m/.

6. Evans, G. and Mellon, J. 'Working Class Votes and Conservative Losses: Solving the UKIP Puzzle', *Parliamentary Affairs,* Volume 6 (3), July 2015 http://pa.oxfordjournals.org/content/early/2015/04/16/pa.gsv005.full

7. Harrop, A. (2015), *The Mountain to Climb: Labour's 2020 Challenge*, London: Fabian Society, http://www.fabians.org.uk/wp-content/uploads/2015/06/The-Mountain-to-Climb1.pdf.

8. Ipsos Mori, 'How Britain Voted in 2015: The 2015 Election – Who Voted for Whom?', Ipsos Mori, 22 May 2015, https://www.ipsos-mori.com/researchpublications/researcharchive/3575/How-Britain-voted-in-2015.

THE ELECTORAL BATTLEGROUND

Polling Analysis and the Views
of Wavering Voters

This chapter presents the quantitative polling research carried out by Ipsos Mori alongside the key findings of our qualitative survey carried out among voters across England, Wales and Scotland.[1] The poll was conducted 10 days before the general election; it provides a snapshot of the electorate's attitudes and views as they weighed up which way to vote in the period up to 7 May.[2] The chapter focuses on voters' perceptions of Labour and examines why so many were not prepared to support the party at the 2015 election.

The results underline the scale of the political challenge now facing Labour in the wake of its election defeat. In 2010, our research for *Southern Discomfort Again* found deep disillusionment after 13 years of Labour government and the financial crisis. Since then, the party appears to have gone backwards: its strategic position is, in key respects, worse than it was five years ago. We found evidence of important differences of social class and geography in voters' attitudes, which partly explains Labour's variable regional performance and its inability to connect with large swathes of England. These voters recognise that Labour has a social conscience and wants to make Britain fairer, but they have little confidence in the party's economic management credentials seven years on from the financial crash. They will not take much notice of Labour's social vision until they can be sure the party will not plunge Britain back into economic chaos.

Britain today is an economically anxious country where faith in politics has fallen to an all-time low. Middle-income, working- and middle-class Britain feels increasingly betrayed, unable to have confidence in any of the established political parties. These voters are aspirant and as anxious to get on in life as ever, but they are cautious about their prospects in the face of rising job insecurity, declining real wages, plummeting living standards and, as a consequence, a major increase in household debt. They want a better future for their children and grandchildren, but worry that life is set to get even tougher and that the advantages of a middle-class lifestyle – a steady, well-paid job, owning your own home, regular foreign holidays, a decent education – will be even harder to attain for the next generation. Middle-income Britain wants hope in the face of pessimism and uncertainty.

LABOUR HAS GONE BACKWARDS SINCE 2010

Labour today is seen as less of a national party than it was in 2010:

- Only one-third of voters (34 per cent) now say that Labour is close to people in the south of England, compared to 55 per cent in 2011 (see Table 2.1). Unsurprisingly, 71 per cent say the Conservatives are close to people in the south.

Table 2.1   Who are Labour and the Tories close to?

	Immigrants		The trade unions		The middle class		Homeowners		People in the south of England	
	2010	2015	2010	2015	2010	2015	2010	2015	2010	2015
Labour	57%	47%	67%	68%	55%	40%	55%	39%	55%	34%
Conservatives	19%	24%	19%	10%	69%	68%	60%	62%	78%	71%

Source: Ipsos Mori for Policy Network

- This is mirrored by a fall in the proportion of voters who say that Labour is close to the middle class, down from 55 per cent in 2010 to 40 per cent today. This compares to 68 per cent for the Conservatives.
- In 2010, Labour and the Conservatives were seen as relatively equal in terms of being close to those who own their own home (55 and 60 per cent respectively). By 2015, the proportion of voters who saw Labour as close to home-owners fell to 39 per cent, while it remained at a similar level (62 per cent) for the Conservatives.
- Labour's pursuit of the '35 per cent strategy' targeting 'core' Labour voters and disaffected left-leaning Liberal Democrats appears to have markedly narrowed its base of support. The party is now perceived as close to the working class by a margin of 62 to 24 per cent.

Despite reforming its links with the trade unions, a similar proportion of voters (68 per cent) perceive Labour to be close to the unions as in 2010 (67 per cent). One area in which Labour has apparently made some progress is in pursuing a tougher stance on immigration. Less than half of voters (47 per cent) now believe that Labour is close to immigrants, compared to 57 per cent in 2010 – then hardly surprising perhaps in the wake of Gordon Brown's travails with Gillian Duffy in Rochdale. The Conservatives are now seen as somewhat closer to immigrants (24 per cent compared to 19 per cent), which is no doubt reflected in rising support for Ukip. When asked whether Labour was more interested in helping immigrants instead of those born in Britain, voters were evenly divided (33 per cent agreed; 33 per cent disagreed). We return to this theme below.

Labour's electoral strength is that many voters would like to trust and support the party: they identify with Labour's broader mission of a fairer society with opportunities widely spread. As one voter said: "I would like to vote Labour next time. They represent my sort of experience more than the Conservatives." Another added: "For me, it's always a struggle not to vote for Labour. I would naturally vote Labour, I voted for Blair and Brown." When Labour had been on the brink of government before, one younger voter felt a sense of optimism about the future: "A couple of times in my life I felt there was some kind of hope, like when you had [Bill] Clinton and Blair. I felt change was possible . . . I am from a strong Labour

THE PARTY OF ECONOMIC INCOMPETENCE

Labour has made little progress since 2010 in addressing its key strategic weakness: a reputation for economic incompetence. Only 16 per cent of voters trust the party most to run the economy – exactly the same figure as in 2010 – compared to 33 per cent for the Tories (in the south-east, the margin is 42 to 11 per cent). In the south of England (outside London), the figure falls to 11 per cent.[3] Just 12 per cent of voters trust Labour most to reduce the budget deficit, the same figure as in 2010 (falling to eight per cent in the south). In the West Midlands, the Conservatives are more trusted than Labour to reduce the deficit by 44 to 10 per cent. The Labour leadership's argument that the deficit was rising under the Conservative chancellor, George Osborne, because of falling real wages (and therefore of declining tax revenues) completely failed to connect with voters.

Since the financial crash, Labour has utterly failed to restore its economic credibility with the

ure was 37 per cent. The voters we interviewed had little sense of what Labour's economic policy actually amounted to. What they did remember was scarcely advantageous to the party's reputation: "There was a sense they were against people who generate wealth."

Labour was still blamed for the crash and the deficit by most of the respondents, and not felt to have policies to deal with the deficit: "They messed things up in 2010. They screwed up on the economy.

Even if they didn't overspend, they didn't put the case well that they didn't overspend." Another voter was adamant: "The Labour attitude to spending was wrong and they were reluctant to admit the Labour government spent too much. They overspent, they were blind about the financial troubles and they don't admit that." Voters wanted Labour to recognise that the deficit was a problem and had to be addressed head on by whoever was in government: "They are anti-austerity and want to continue spending and I agree with the Conservative policy of paying off the debt. That is essential and I disagree with Labour. You've got to try and pay it back; you've got to take that seriously. I mean, look at the mess they made. And they left the Conservatives to deal with it and we are all still paying for that."

Nonetheless, the Conservatives were scarcely applauded for their economic performance: trust in them to run the economy fell from 44 per cent to 33 per cent between 2010 and 2015 reflecting the anaemic recovery and the stagnation of wages and living standards. Osborne missed his government's deficit reduction targets: as a result, trust in the Conservatives to reduce the budget deficit fell from 51 per cent in 2010 to 35 per cent by 2015. That said the Conservatives were notably more trusted on the deficit in southern England (40 per cent).

The mood in Britain remains markedly pessimistic seven years after the financial crisis first struck. When asked "whether children growing up in Britain today are likely to face a tougher time as adults than their parents' generation", 68 per cent agreed against seven per cent who disagreed. A majority were not confident their children or grandchildren would be as secure financially (51 to 40 per cent), able to fulfil their educational potential without incurring large debts (64 to 28 per cent), or to buy a home before they are thirty (69 to 23 per cent). The electorate's attitude today is stoic but hardly upbeat: 32 per cent expect life to be tough but they will get by; 30 per cent think they'll be "just about ok". Those currently in work were less confident they would find a job if made redundant (46 to 36 per cent), but people in the south of England are unsurprisingly somewhat more optimistic.

One voter, referring to the acute sense of economic insecurity among those on middle incomes, said: "My friends have kids and they spend a phenomenal amount of money to break even at the end of the month and they can't even go on holiday. If you work hard you should be able to go on holiday. They can't. People I know are working 60 hours a week and are still having to claim tax credits. That is unbelievable. It makes people tired and not engaged with politics." There was a feeling that the worst might now be over although life was still tough: "It's better than it was but we do struggle. We're always worried about paying the bills and we don't have anything extra left over." The so-called 'squeeze' on middle incomes had been felt acutely: "I have not had a pay rise for 20 years. My husband earns less than he did 20 years ago. My rate of pay is the same as it was in 1988. The only thing that has gone up is the prices." Labour identified the salient issue of the 'squeezed middle' after 2010, but given the perception of economic incompetence the party was not trusted to remedy the problem. Labour's campaign rhetoric focusing on zero-hours contracts highlighted issues that generally affect those on very low incomes rather than the middle.

THE LEADERSHIP QUESTION

Being leader of the opposition is a tough job, especially given the hostile media. However, the tracking surveys conducted by YouGov demonstrated that Ed Miliband was never trusted or liked by voters. Even towards the end of the election campaign, during which he was generally believed to have performed well, he was thought to be doing badly by 56 per cent of voters. This was better than at the beginning of the year, when 70 per cent thought he was doing badly. After a brief honeymoon from when he was elected leader until April 2011, his 'doing badly' rating has hardly been below 50 per cent. Similarly, YouGov figures between 2010 and 2015 show that Miliband never got above the mid-20s when voters were asked who would make the best prime minister. Cameron, although not liked, was always between 30 to 40 per cent.[4]

The last YouGov tracker before the election, taken on 4–5 May, showed the following views about Miliband and Cameron:

Table 2.2   Miliband v Cameron: voters' views on leaders' characteristics

Leaders' characteristics	Miliband %	Cameron %
Sticks to what he believes in	23	27
Honest	19	12
Strong	9	21
In touch with ordinary people	26	8
Good in a crisis	5	19
Decisive	9	24
A natural leader	4	21
Charismatic	6	17
None of these	49	41
Don't know	11	8

Source: YouGov Tracker Poll, 4–5 May 2015

Although at the end of the campaign Miliband was perceived to be more honest and in touch with ordinary people than Cameron, he only scored in single figures on the key leadership qualities of 'being good in a crisis', 'decisive' and 'a natural leader'. Miliband sought to project himself as a conviction politician, but he was actually seen as less principled than Cameron, perhaps as a consequence of his transactional, focus group-driven approach to politics.

YouGov's results are not unique: all the polling companies showed similarly dire results for Miliband: Ipsos Mori's 'Political Trends' demonstrate that he was not regarded as capable enough to be prime minister. In November 2014, they found that only 13 per cent believed that Miliband was ready to be prime minister, while 73 per cent thought he was not. That finding included the majority of Labour supporters: 53 per cent said he was not ready to be prime minister with only 35 per cent saying he was.[5] By February 2015, the numbers saying he was ready had risen, but only to 21 per cent, while 63 per cent still disagreed.[6] In March 2015, Ipsos Mori found that 30 per cent agreed with the statement: "I do not like

Ed Miliband but I like the Labour party", while 32 per cent liked neither Ed Miliband nor the Labour party.[7] In April, only 33 per cent thought he was a capable leader and 24 per cent that he would be good in a crisis. Similarly, ICM's polls consistently found that voters thought Miliband was doing a poor job.[8]

The verdict of our qualitative survey was equally damning: "I didn't like Miliband. If you have no confidence in the leader, then you're thinking: what are they going to do in power?" Some voters were more sympathetic given the mauling Labour's leader received from the press: "He's always fighting against a tide of being unconvincing although he's probably a good guy. His heart is in the right place." However, others objected to the manner of Miliband's leadership victory in 2010: "Ed Miliband was the wrong leader, he came in with union support and has been deluded and eccentric . . . He didn't fill me with confidence or make me believe in him or the Labour party and I really, really disliked Ed Balls . . . They got the wrong Miliband." There was a feeling that Labour's leadership team were rather stale and unable to present a fresh vision to the country: "The old guard like Ed Balls are past their sell-by date . . . Ed Balls was not the right sort of man. The Conservatives ran rings round them."

It was also significant that Miliband's ratings were lower than those of the Labour party itself. In the months before the election, *The Independent* reported that: "Most polls still have Miliband hovering around the −20 per cent mark (a stark improvement over this time three or four months ago, when he was nearer −40 per cent in some approval ratings) and only Survation report that the Labour leader has ventured into the positives."[9] The leadership question also blunted Labour's response to the accusation that it would be in a weak coalition government with the SNP at the mercy of Nicola Sturgeon: "The biggest concern I had was the SNP having a significant influence in a coalition government and using that influence, so although I disagree with a lot of what the Conservatives stood for, I would rather have a Conservative government able to stand up to the SNP."

WHAT DOES LABOUR STAND FOR?

One apparent success of Miliband's period as leader was to convey a sharper sense of what Labour stands for (see Figure 2.1). In 2011, only 40 per cent of voters were clear what Labour stood for in comparison to 58 per cent by 2015 (while 36 per cent were unclear). In the south of England, the figure rose from 37 per cent to 59 per cent. Intriguingly, Scottish voters were less clear about what Labour stood for in 2015: the figures here were 54 to 41 per cent. The problem, however, was that although voters overall felt they knew more about Labour, they did not particularly like what they heard.

Labour's leader developed a succession of arguments such as his attack on predatory capitalists and energy companies, while railing against the excesses of the wealthy. Voters knew more about what Miliband stood for, but it worried them or actively deterred them from supporting Labour. They also felt that Labour lacked a positive appeal and message, spending too much time attacking the other parties: "There was no clear message apart from being oppositional." Labour is seen as a party that no longer has the confidence to stand up for what it believes in: "They're not courageous. They don't say what they think." Younger votes in Scotland particularly

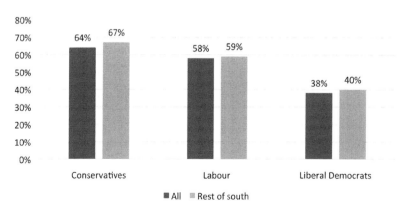

Figure 2.1 **Voters that are clear what the major parties stand for.** *Source*: Ipsos Mori for Policy Network

felt that Labour had failed to set out a convincing alternative: "I was disappointed that Labour didn't distance themselves from the cuts. Welfare has been used as a scapegoat. Labour could have pointed that out. We heard the SNP saying they would fight for our interests. What did Labour say? Keep voting Labour and you get the cuts."

Moreover, even more voters were clear what the Conservatives stood for in 2015 at 64 per cent than the 29 per cent who were not clear (the figures were 67 to 28 per cent in the south of England and 66 to 28 per cent in the West Midlands – there was no significant difference with the rest of Britain). Although repetitive and in key respects disingenuous, the message about the Conservatives' long-term economic plan clearly struck home. The Liberal Democrats evidently suffered because after five years in coalition attempting to moderate the Tories' more extreme policies, voters lost a clear sense of what the party was about.

LABOUR'S IMAGE IN THE MINDS OF VOTERS

As we have seen, voters across Britain do not trust Labour on the economy. They see Labour as an incompetent party which they are reluctant to trust with their own money. Only 14 per cent of voters in southern England perceive Labour to be "forward-looking", and just four per cent believe it would keep its promises. Too many voters believe that Labour is a backward-looking party trapped in a mind-set of heavy industry and the cloth cap: "They're ineffective, they're old-fashioned. They're living in a world where it was them and the Conservatives . . . they are outdated and they don't know reality." This is combined with a lack of confidence in Labour's ability to govern. By 45 to 22 per cent, voters perceive Labour negatively rather than positively: in the West Midlands, the margin is 50 to 23 per cent, and in the south of England, it is 52 to 17 per cent. Among C2 voters who were the cornerstone of Labour's success in 1997, 2001 and 2005, Labour is seen negatively by 48 to 19 per cent.

The one positive finding is that, unlike in the 1980s and early 1990s, Labour is not seen as more "extreme" than the Conservatives, perhaps reflecting Tory splits over Europe, as well as the severity of the government's austerity programme. However, the electorate do not believe that Labour would get a grip on issues like welfare and social responsibility. By 44 to 20 per cent, voters believe the party is "not really serious about tackling the 'something for nothing culture'". Those in the south-east of England (48 agree to 16 per cent who disagree) and C2 social class voters (46 to 17 per cent) are even more sceptical. Worryingly, Labour is seen as not as close to older voters – who are, after all, more likely to turn out and vote – than the Tories (44 per cent see the party as close to the over 65s and 38 per cent do not, compared to 49 to 35 per cent for the Conservatives).

Labour is still seen as the party which best understands and represents ordinary people, although this strategic advantage is under threat from Ukip. Across Britain, 23 per cent of voters say Labour is the most representative party, and 21 per cent say it best understands ordinary people. This is compared to 15 per cent to 14 per cent for Ukip and 10 to 11 per cent for the Conservatives. Labour is also seen as closer to women (45 to 35 per cent compared to 35 to 46 for the Tories on a measure of "close/not close"). People trust Labour to act more "fairly" than the Conservatives on taxes and welfare benefits by 28 to 21 per cent, and to help those who are struggling and want to get on by 29 to 18 per cent.

The party is seen as more likely to understand people's concerns about day-to-day life than the Tories (by 27 to 16 per cent). Labour is also ahead as the party best placed to ensure value for money in public services by 26 to 21 per cent (although in south-east England it is the Conservatives who are ahead by 31 to 19 per cent). However, voters believe that the Tories rather than Labour are more likely to get "good value for taxpayers' money" by 21 to 15 per cent (the figures are 24 to 12 per cent in the West Midlands and 25 to 12 per cent in the south). The Conservatives are no less trusted than Labour to cut spending fairly (19 to 18 per cent;

22 to 14 per cent in the West Midlands). The voters our qualitative research team interviewed for this study were adamant that Labour no longer empathises with the middle classes in today's Britain: "They don't understand the middle classes like us – educated people on our uppers. We've got degrees coming out of our ears but we're poor. We've bankrupted ourselves to educate our children." This was confirmed by the sense that Labour had significantly narrowed its electoral appeal: "They want to say they stand for working-class people and this has been pushed hard on them by the trade unions.

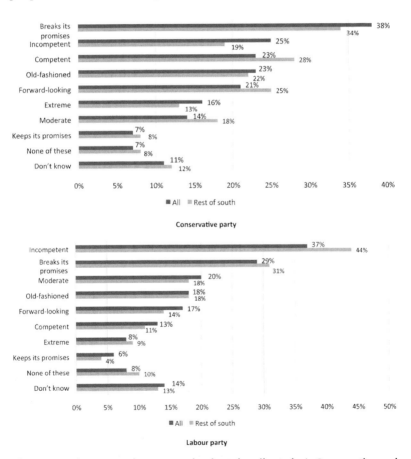

Figure 2.2 The two or three terms that best describe today's Conservative and Labour parties. *Source*: Ipsos Mori for Policy Network

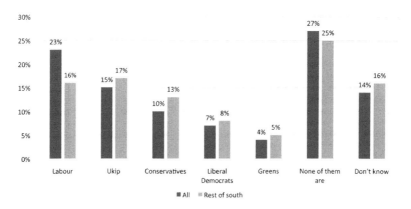

Figure 2.3 Party most representative of ordinary people. *Source*: Ipsos Mori for Policy Network

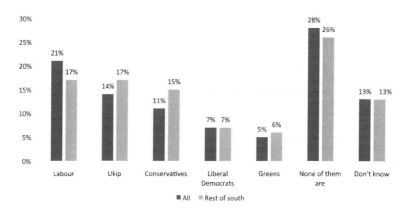

Figure 2.4 Party that best understands the problems of ordinary people. *Source*: Ipsos Mori for Policy Network

It's got to be wider than the poor in society." Another added: "I think I associate them with minorities of all sorts."

The dominant mood in Britain today is one of 'anti-politics': voters are more likely to say that none of the parties are representative and understand ordinary people. The Conservatives have major weaknesses in their party image – a further reason why their overall majority in 2015 was so unexpected and, indeed, so calamitous for Labour. Voters have a "negative" rather than a "positive" view of the Conservatives by 46 to 26 per cent, as against 45 to 22 per cent for Labour. The British electorate by 57 to 17 per cent agree that "the Conservatives are more interested in looking after the rich than the British people as a whole." They are perceived to be close to privileged groups such as the rich by 81 to six per cent, and to "businessmen and the City" by 79 to seven per cent. By 45 to 26 per cent, voters believed the Tories were "not really serious" about protecting the National Health Service, underlining that the NHS remains a major vulnerability for the Conservative party. As Peter Kellner puts it: "The most devastating fact about the general election for Labour (or maybe the second most devastating fact, after its collapse in Scotland) is that the Tories achieved an overall majority despite being seen as the party of the rich with little concern for ordinary voters."[10]

LABOUR AND FAIRNESS

It is astonishing that despite never using the language of 'equality', voters believe the Conservatives are just as likely to achieve equality as Labour in southern England by 18 per cent to 15 per cent (as Figures 2.5 and 2.6 record). Nearly one-quarter of voters in the south (24 per cent) trust the Tories to achieve social mobility compared to only 14 per cent who trust Labour. During the Thatcher years, the Conservatives clearly established themselves in the south as the party best placed to ensure upward mobility and rising aspiration. Across Britain, Labour is the most trusted of all the parties on equality (20 per cent) compared to the Conservatives (14 per cent), but the parties are almost tied on who voters trust most to achieve social mobility (18 per cent to 17 per cent).

   This result is a calamity for a party such as Labour which is ostensibly committed to radical equality of opportunity, breaking down the barriers that hold people back. It is the Tories who ought to be seen as the party of the privileged few given the extraordinary number of Old Etonians in the cabinet, a point even Michael Gove could

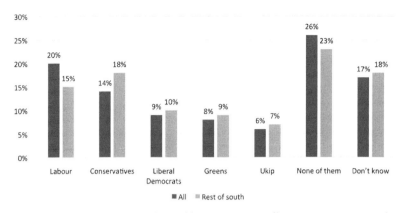

Figure 2.5 Party most trusted to achieve greater equality. *Source*: Ipsos Mori for Policy Network

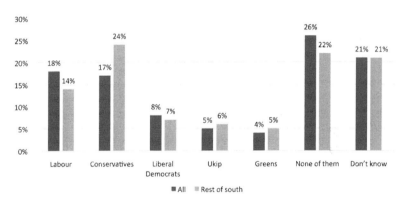

Figure 2.6 Party most trusted to achieve greater social mobility. *Source*: Ipsos Mori for Policy Network

not resist recently making.[11] Labour's difficulty is that voters do not identify with the concept of fairness – helping people at the top and bottom of society and ignoring the struggling middle – which they think the party now believes in: "Ordinary people are hauled through the courts for benefit fraud but look at the bankers and politicians' expenses ... They [Labour] only want fairness for some people, like people on benefits and low wages but they don't think about

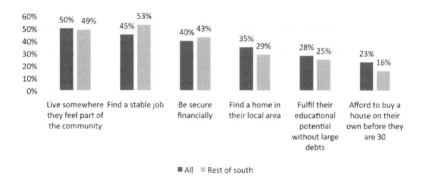

Figure 2.7   Those confident in their children's/grandchildren's future by aspiration. *Source*: Ipsos Mori for Policy Network

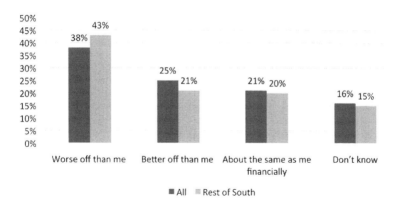

Figure 2.8   Expectations of children's/grandchildren's future living standards. *Source*: Ipsos Mori for Policy Network

the rest." Another voter was equally unequivocal: "It's not fair that people on benefits get more than I do working."

The strategic opportunity for Labour is that voters across Britain, particularly in the south of England, tend to be pessimistic about young people's ability in the future to own their home and enjoy a decent standard of living. Only 16 per cent of southern voters are confident that their children or grandchildren will be able to afford to buy a home on their own by the age of 30. Indeed, 43 per cent of

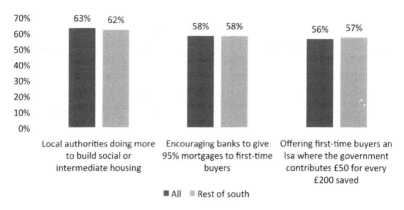

Figure 2.9 Support for specific policies to widen home ownership. *Source*: Ipsos Mori for Policy Network

southern voters believe their children or grandchildren will be worse off (compared to 38 per cent across Great Britain).

There was also a striking degree of support for the government's housing policies: 58 per cent of British voters back the government's right-to-buy mortgage deposit scheme, which is opposed by only 16 per cent. Fifty-six per cent endorse the government's help-to-buy ISA (opposed by 14 per cent), a policy especially popular in the West Midlands (62 to 13 per cent). However, there is greatest support for giving local authorities additional resources to build more social and intermediate housing by 63 per cent to eight per cent. There was a real sense that the housing system did not work for ordinary people: "All the housing has been sold off and it's impossible to afford", said one voter. Another complained: "Young people can't even think about buying a house. There's too many people jumping the queue and getting housing and the people who pay private rents just keep paying more and more." Britain is perceived as a country where the chance to get on and own your own home or find a secure tenancy is increasingly a privilege of the elite few.

There was also considerable unease about the impact of tuition fees in university education making it harder for young people to get degrees and burdening future generations with debt: "I've got children who are grown up and gone to university and got hammered by university fees. Labour introduced that and they've gone up and up." Another parent bemoaned Labour's failure to widen the range of opportunities available for young people: "My son has a £25,000 loan and he'll never pay it off. Labour brought that in just so people could have stupid degrees. They should have had more imagination about widening higher education, like apprenticeships." If Labour were actually trusted on the economy, it might be taken more seriously as an advocate of equal opportunity and social mobility.

LABOUR AND PUBLIC SERVICES

Labour in 2015 sought to attack the Conservatives for undermining public services by imposing indiscriminate cuts, particularly in local government and policing. However, the electorate were not particularly receptive to the message as Figure 2.10 indicates. Forty-four per cent of voters believe that "spending restrictions and cuts have reduced waste in public services", compared to 32 per cent who say it has not (although 59 per cent believed the cuts had

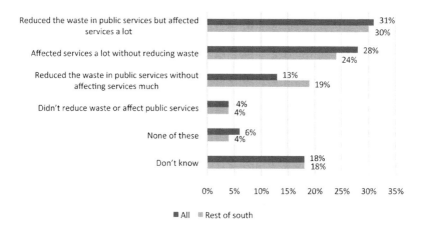

Figure 2.10   The impact of spending restrictions and cuts. *Source*: Ipsos Mori for Policy Network

affected services overall). In the south, the figures are 49 per cent to 28 per cent. Overall, the public disagree that it is possible to cut spending in areas such as health, education and the police without reducing the quality of services (by 41 to 28 per cent), although voters in the south (39 to 27 per cent) and C2 working-class voters (39 to 26 per cent) were marginally less sympathetic.

POPULAR ATTITUDES TO IMMIGRATION

Immigration is now regarded as one of the most potent issues in British political debate. It remains an important concern for voters throughout Great Britain. Much of this is to do with employment and living standards. People disagree that immigration is needed to do jobs that British workers will not do by 50 to 36 per cent. They believe that immigrants are undercutting indigenous British workers and forcing down wages (by 55 to 30 per cent). C2 working-class voters are especially concerned about the impact of wage under-cutting (60 to 26 per cent). These voters also feel that too much pressure has been placed on public services and infrastructure: "Immigration may be good for the job market but not for everyone else. This place is overcrowded. Our local school is full of people from Poland. I can't get doctors' appointments." Another voter added: "There are a lot of people very resentful about people coming in and needing housing and getting in front of other people."

In relation to cultural identity, 64 per cent of voters agree that Britain has been too ready to "change the rules to suit immigrants", and by 48 to 39 per cent they believe that immigration "is destroying our culture and way of life". The views of voters in our qualitative survey on this point are stark: "The immigration thing is a catastrophe. Our social make-up completely altered in a decade. No one speaks English on the bus." There was a widespread feeling that the failure to manage immigration was a legacy of the previous Labour government: "Labour was very slow to deal with immigration. People are generous here, we don't mind people coming in, but we are a small island, our infrastructure can't cope. Politicians felt it was a race issue and ordinary people felt they didn't understand their view." They objected to the fact Labour never really appeared to understand the problem and as one voter put it, were determined to, "rub their noses in diversity".

This fuelled the rise in support for Ukip in 2015: "Ukip are not beyond the pale, they say things working people can relate to, Labour doesn't understand that. No wonder people voted Ukip. A million babies have been born, immigrant children, and they didn't think about that when they were in government. Go down to the pub and listen to what people are saying, that's what Ukip did well." According to Rob Ford from the University of Manchester, Ukip voters are more likely to be those without formal educational qualifications (more so than being classified as working class). Ukip do best in seats with a relatively low proportion of public sector workers and BME voters, and which have recently experienced a sharp rise in inward migration from EU accession countries; Ford argues that support for Ukip is correlated more strongly with cultural attitudes to immigration than with either hostility to the EU or support for traditional redistribution.

Nonetheless, attitudes to immigration are not overwhelmingly negative. There was a feeling among younger voters that fears about immigration might be based on a "myth": "I don't know the answer to what's happening, how can I? How can anyone? I don't know if what we read is all a myth. I know the Conservatives are always talking about stopping it." Sixty-eight per cent believe that Britain should encourage "hard-working immigrants" who wish to contribute to the country (18 per cent disagree).

By a margin of 47 to 36 per cent, voters agree that immigrants provide "healthy competition" for British workers "by doing quality work at reasonable prices". Fifty-two per cent affirm that immigration has given Britain a "varied and vibrant culture" (35 per cent disagree). Voters disagree by 61 to 29 per cent that "British people seem like a minority in my area", although in the West Midlands that margin shrinks to 56 to 35 per cent. Scottish voters are considerably more positive about immigration: for example, they are less likely to agree that immigration is "destroying our culture" (47 to 45 per cent). There was a feeling that where problems have occurred it was due to rapid migration flows and cuts in public infrastructure: "There's a lot of scapegoating around immigration. I live in Bristol and a lot of strain we are seeing is about reduction of services not immigration. There is a pull on resources not because of immigration, but because of cuts in funding."

DEMOCRACY AND THE NEW POLITICS

There is an appetite among voters for substantive political reform. One of the factors that has driven citizens away from supporting the mainstream parties is dissatisfaction with the system of democracy in Britain. There is a strong perception that the political class cannot be trusted: "I feel they betrayed young people so badly, the whole lot of them. This is the mess they've created, the political class don't admit to the mess they've made. They're alright and they can bugger off and earn millions. They don't have humility because they're in this little bubble and they're fine." Many politicians are now held in contempt: "People feel politicians are in it for themselves . . . you just feel it's a bit of a gravy train. There are too many of them who don't have experience outside politics."

As a result, a majority across Britain would like to see reform of the electoral system so that "minority parties are better represented" (49 to 14 per cent), although the proposal in a referendum to adopt the alternative vote was defeated in 2011. One voter responded: "A lot of people didn't vote but it didn't represent people not want-ing to vote, it reflected people not thinking their vote counted. If you know there'll be some representation, people would want to vote." Giving more powers to local authorities in areas such as housing and health is supported by 51 to 13 per cent. A proposal to remove the remaining hereditary peers in the House of Lords is backed by 46 to 12 per cent of voters. There is some support for the creation of an

English parliament "along the lines of the Scottish parliament" by 35 to 18 per cent (interestingly, Scottish voters support an English parliament by 40 to 13 per cent).

There are major obstacles to Labour projecting itself as a party of the new politics, however, not least the sense among voters that it does not yet have its own house in order. As one voter remarked: "I'm worried about the influence of Len McCluskey, he's trying to bully the Labour party and threaten to withdraw funding if they don't choose the right candidate." There was a real sense that changes in British politics posed major challenges for the Labour party: "We're going to multi-party politics now and that's very difficult for Labour." There is some appetite for a more radical approach in recasting the landscape of British politics: "It's never going to happen, but they could align themselves with the other parties – the Liberals and the Greens – and say 'we want the country to be governed this way'."

SUMMARY

Our research confirms that voters across Britain today live in fear of profligacy and waste after seven years of recession and economic stagnation. They are not unsympathetic to Labour's wider aspirations for a fairer and more compassionate society, but they will not listen properly to the party until it has re-established its reputation on the core issue of economic competence. In a more volatile and uncertain world, voters are in no mood to take risks over who is elected to govern the country. Voters are actually very clear about what they want from Labour: "They've got to have a competent leader and people have to trust them to run the economy." There was a strong sense that Britain needs an electable Labour party: "Labour is needed because you don't want the Conservatives in forever screwing up working people. Labour needs to get a good leader, make it clear they get what people want and are concerned about – the cost of education, housing and the cost of living."

Our poll demonstrates that Labour did make some progress after 2010 in reassuring voters on the issue of immigration and in rebuilding its links to the working class. The notion that Labour's recovery will be achieved by appealing only to traditional working-class voters and by toughening Labour's line on immigration ought to be treated with scepticism. That is what the party has done for much of the last five years. There is little to be gained by trying to out-Ukip Ukip. The key to winning back trust and reassuring voters on immigration is the economy. Labour needs to show that it will run the economy sensibly, while at the same time tackling the root causes of economic insecurity in a way that does not cost jobs and competitiveness. The strategic priority now is to widen significantly Labour's base of electoral support in the country.

NOTES

1. The interviews were carried out with voters in marginal seats by a Policy Network qualitative research team on the telephone and face-to-face between mid-May and mid-July 2015.

2. The poll was carried out online by Ipsos Mori from 24th-28th April on British adults aged 18–75. Data is weighted to match the population profile 2015. Further details of the poll are available directly from Ipsos Mori. http://www.ipsos-mori.com

3. In this report, references to voters in the south of England and southern England exclude London.

4. https://d25d2506sfb94s.cloudfront.net/cumulus_uploads/document/7rj2tjjm1c/YG-Archives-Pol-Trackers-Leaders-Perceptions-050515.pdf.

5. Ipsos Mori, 'Labour Support Lowest Since Before 2010 General Election', Ipsos Mori, 12 November 2014, https://www.ipsos-mori.com/researchpublications/researcharchive/3475/Labour-support-lowest-since-before-2010-general-election.

6. Ipsos Mori, 'Is . . . Ready to be Prime Minister?', Ipsos Mori, 12 February 2015, https://www.ipsos-mori.com/researchpublications/researcharchive/2401/Is-Ready-to-be-Prime-Minister-Trends-1994-present.

7. Ipsos Mori, 'Labour are the Most Popular Party, but Miliband Trails Behind', Ipsos Mori, 16 March 2015, https://www.ipsos-mori.com/

researchpublications/researcharchive/3541/Labour-are-the-most-popular-party-but-Miliband-trails-behind.

8. Boon, M. 'Guardian Leaders' Poll – October 2014', ICM Unlimited, 8 October 2014, http://www.icmunlimited.com/media-centre/polls/guardian-poll-october-2014.

9. Embley, J. 'Where Are Ed Miliband, Nigel Farage and David Cameron in the Latest Opinion Polls?', *The Independent*, 22 April 2015, http://www.independent.co.uk/news/uk/politics/generalelection/where-are-ed-miliband-nigel-farage-and-david-cameron-in-the-latest-opinion-polls-10194316.html.

10. Kellner, P. 'Rock Bottom', *Progress*, 4 June 2015, http://www.progressonline.org.uk/2015/06/04/rock-bottom-2/.

11. Wintour, P. 'Gove Attacks "Preposterous" Number of Old Etonians in Cameron's Cabinet', *The Guardian*, 14 March 2014, http://www.theguardian.com/politics/2014/mar/14/gove-attacks-preposterous-number-old-etonians-cameron-cabinet.

WHY LABOUR LOST

Party Views

This chapter examines why Labour lost from the unique perspective of candidates, key campaigners and party workers in the 2015 election. The survey of Labour candidates and activists carried out for this study reveals that the party understood it was in much bigger trouble on the ground than was acknowledged nationally ahead of the election. While opinion polls had pointed towards Labour at least becoming the largest party in a minority or coalition government, activists at local level were much more sceptical. Even before the election campaign commenced, it was clear that Labour would be irreparably damaged by the toxic combination of an unpopular leader who voters did not believe could be prime minister and the party's weak ratings on economic competence.

To find out why Labour did so badly across the country, we conducted interviews with key campaigners in seats that Labour failed to win in 2015 including Stockton South, Carlisle, Sherwood, Lincoln, Cannock Chase, Ipswich, Harlow, Southampton Itchen, and Stroud. Most of these marginal seats are located in the Midlands and southern England. Many had been expected to fall to Labour relatively easily: none were in affluent Tory areas; Labour had held these constituencies for much of the period it was in government between 1997 and 2010; and most of the seats had successful Labour councils that were popular locally. Substantial resources had also been invested as part of Labour's key seats strategy and there were many outstanding candidates.

Yet these seats were lost at the general election, often with significantly increased Tory majorities. Of course, there were particular factors at work in local constituencies such as a rise in support for Ukip driven by a high rate of inward migration from EU accession countries; this hit Labour badly. However, the principal reason why Labour lost these seats was because swing voters ultimately opted to vote Tory. At a time of constitutional uncertainty following the Scottish independence referendum and economic insecurity following the worst financial crisis since the 1930s, voters were ultimately not prepared to trust Ed Miliband's Labour party.

There were, however, some seats where Labour did win against the national tide. We spoke to Labour candidates in constituencies where the party was successful despite the dysfunctional national campaign, notably in Hove and Portslade, Exeter, and Ilford North, to understand why Labour was victorious. Learning lessons from those successes will be crucial in planning the next general election campaign.

WHY DID LABOUR LOSE?

There was wide-ranging agreement as to the reasons for Labour's defeat: the views of candidates and activists are similar to those of the voters. Labour lost because it was not trusted to run the economy; it was perceived to have a weak leader who the public did not believe could be prime minister; and Labour failed to put forward either a compelling policy prospectus for the future, or a positive, uplifting national message that could provide the country with a sense of common purpose. Furthermore, the Conservatives successfully defined the 2015 election as a choice about the economy and leadership rather than a verdict on five years of coalition government.

Miliband was not as disliked as Gordon Brown had been in 2010 and was perceived to have performed reasonably well during the 'short' campaign, but there was little trust in, or respect for, Miliband among the party faithful. One candidate was clear about the impact of an unpopular leader: "Ed Miliband was a big issue on the doorstep – they didn't take to him. From that, the Tories could use the SNP and other things. He's a perfectly nice man but voters didn't like him at all. Partly it was a superficial dislike because we are fed this diet of celebrity. The media had an enormous influence on the public. If I had a pound for every person who said, 'You picked the wrong brother', I'd be rich, but actually they wouldn't recognise him [David Miliband] if they fell over him on the street."

There was a strong feeling even among the candidates that Miliband simply lacked the gravitas and credibility to be prime minister: "Ed never did it on the doorstep, he was particularly unpopular with men, they never saw him as a prime minister . . . He came across better in the campaign but people had already made up their mind. It just confirmed he was an OK guy, it didn't win any votes." According to opinion research, Miliband did not only lose because he was too ideologically 'leftwing' for British voters – in the end, he lost because he was Ed Miliband.[1]

Since Labour's leader was not regarded as a plausible prime minister, the Tories were able to intensify their attack on a Labour-SNP coalition government in which Miliband would be 'held to ransom' by Sturgeon. This gave the Conservatives crucial momentum in the final phase of the election campaign: "Our feeling is that people did change at the last minute. I can't be sure how much effect it had but I think it had a big effect. The threat of the SNP was big and linked into the fear of voting Labour." Another candidate added: "The last minute attack about the SNP was effective because it built on previous criticism of Labour – for example, if you were worried about Miliband not being strong enough."

Like our survey of voters, there was a strong feeling among candidates and party activists that Labour in 2015 had too little to say to middle Britain: "I don't think they knew what our offer was.

The idea was, 'we've gone through five years of pain and it's getting better, so we'll stick with the Tories'. There was a whole load of people we didn't have anything to say to: if they were earning over £8 an hour and didn't have 3–4 year-olds needing childcare, what did we have to say to them?" Labour campaigned hard on the message that the Conservatives had made life tougher for working people after five years of austerity, but this did not sit easily with the experience of most voters: "People didn't feel as badly off as our message was – they were thinking, 'well, it is bad but it's not that bad.' A lot of undecideds up to the last week said, 'I'd really like to vote Labour but I can't.' People went into the polling station wanting to vote for us and they just couldn't. People blamed us for the deficit – 'look what happened last time you were in' – all those lines came straight from the Tories."

Since 2010, Labour's message about the country's prospects had been predominantly negative. Of course, some families have been made significantly worse off by changes in social security benefits, the so-called bedroom tax and cuts in public services. Nonetheless, Labour's critique of the coalition government's 'austerity' did not chime with the views of the majority of voters who, by May 2015, could detect at least a glimmer of hope and economic recovery on the horizon.

THE POLICY ISSUES

There was a strong feeling among the candidates that Labour had made little progress in winning back its reputation for economic competence after the 2008 crash: "People didn't want the Conservatives, but there was a lot of fear about Labour and the economy . . . They talked of the mess made by Labour and said we bankrupted the country." The collective memory of Labour's economic record is far from positive: "Many people still connect Labour with the recession even though the economic upturn isn't reaching everyone . . . They thought we were anti-business." As a result, confidence in Labour's ability to govern was very low: "Even if we had the discussion and they agreed with us, they still didn't trust us . . . Nationally, they didn't trust us on the economy. They said we were reckless last time round, it was not all our fault but we cocked it up on our watch . . . The problem with the economy hasn't just come up in the last two or three years." The Conservatives had been relentless in contrasting Labour's legacy on the economy with their "long-term economic plan".

Almost all the candidates and party organisers mentioned the issue of immigration as increasing economic insecurity and anxiety among voters, particularly with the key group of C2 and DE voters in the skilled and semi-skilled manual occupations. There was a strong feeling that Labour was simply not prepared to listen to voters on tough issues like immigration because the party was not comfortable with criticism of migration policy or cultural diversity: "Immigration was a big issue . . . It was more talked about by the working classes and lower middle classes. They would say that there were too many immigrants, Labour had let everyone in and it didn't matter if you argued about it, they would carry it on and say this is why there were queues for doctor's appointments and a housing crisis, and why everyone was finding it hard to get a job. Any resources deficit you could imagine was laid at the feet of immigration." This anxiety about immigration was inevitably linked to the previous Labour government's legacy: "They talked about changing communities and changing society – I don't think it was a deciding factor but it helped that people didn't trust us – they said that it was the Labour government that let foreigners in, it was Tony Blair that started immigration." Another candidate from a marginal seat in southern England added: "People didn't see us as the party of working people anymore; they saw us as the party of immigrants." Immigration fuels distrust of the wider political system if voters do not feel they are allowed to discuss contentious issues and that they are 'talked down to' by politicians.

The candidates in 2015 also felt that their efforts were stymied by the lack of a clear, compelling national message: "There were lots and lots of little things but nothing central. Where we said things like about the bedroom tax, people agreed with us but it wasn't enough . . . There wasn't that killer thing to push people over. When people said 'what are you going to do for me?' there was no one policy you could point to – it was just, 'we're not going to kill the NHS', 'not have the bedroom tax', but there was nothing positive." This is confirmed by research carried out for the British Election Study, which found that while the Tories focused attention continually on the economy, Labour had no clear issue strategy and tended to flip day by day from policy theme to policy theme.[2] Labour did have policy positions that might appeal to middle-ground voters, but was unwilling to publicise or communicate them effectively: "We didn't emphasise our popular policies enough, such as scrapping stamp duty for homes under £300,000 and cutting taxes for working people." In Scotland, meanwhile, the impact of having no clear political message or forward policy programme was disastrous: "We didn't have a message for them. There was no real message to counteract the appeal of the SNP."

Where Labour did make a political argument it focused on the state of the NHS. Most voters were not angry with the coalition government's handling of the NHS, however: "People's personal experiences of the NHS were often good, and longer term they don't trust any parties." While voters were not convinced that Labour's policy on the NHS was any better than the Tories, they also felt that Labour lacked the credibility to see through its promises: "The NHS was not enough to make them vote Labour – they didn't think the Tories would wreck the NHS. People felt Labour would look after the NHS better, but it was like other things – a lot of people believed in intervention in the energy companies and so on, but they didn't think we could do it. It was a problem of credibility". Labour was seen as a party which had lots of populist messages but lacked robust, well thought through policies that could actually be implemented in government: "Zero-hour contracts, the bedroom tax position, the NHS and so on went down well as individual policies, but there was no specific messaging on it. It's like *Question Time*, if you mention it, you get a clap, but there's no policy." Meanwhile, voters continued to rank the economy and immigration as the most salient issues, well ahead of the NHS.[3]

A FLAWED ELECTORAL STRATEGY?

Despite these criticisms, in most seats there was little sense of open hostility to Labour: people believed Labour's heart was in the right place, but the mood was one of total lack of confidence in the party according to candidates and party workers. Voters agreed that Labour was compassionate and wanted to help the least fortunate in society, but sensed that Labour lacked the competence and credibility to be a trusted party of government: "Our message was fundamentally rejected by the English people. We relied a lot on heart instead of head. We seemed quite nice about zero-hours contracts, but that's not enough." To be a credible contender for power, Labour has to combine empathy, understanding and concern for others with strength, toughness and reliability: "Traditionally, the Tories have been the party of strength and we have been the party of compassion. The party that wins is the one that can do both. We have to answer difficult questions like immigration and welfare, that's part of being strong, you can't just rely on public services."

As a consequence of being seen as a nice, but fundamentally weak, party, middle-income Britain in 2015 was unwilling to put its trust and confidence in Labour: "The switchers – the lower middle class who would have voted Blair – turned completely against us. The people who were doing OK, they had no link with the Labour party at all. They thought we were going to harm them. Our constituency is very different to how it used to be. They didn't see us as a party that would let them get on, would even stop them getting on. They thought we were the party of people on benefits."

As such, Labour evidently lacked a message that would appeal to the aspirant majority in Britain: "Our literature was good but people said, 'You don't have anything to say to the middle earners' – it was all about zero-hours contracts and the bedroom tax. Those people have to be seduced, they're from working-class backgrounds and they've done well. Their heads say they should vote Tory and their hearts say Labour, and we didn't pull them over the line." Labour was not seen to be on the side of those who were doing well and wanted to get on in life: "We had no narrative compelling for people in work, doing well, we had no message for them. Those people in work, who are doing OK, they want a bigger house, a better car and a better holiday. What could I tell them? What could I offer them? People who want to have a nice car and a holiday, that was the group we needed to engage with and we failed to do that." Labour tended to speak to those at the extremes but not the broader middle class: "The people in the middle, who are not doing that well, but are not hit by the bedroom tax, zero-hour contracts and so on, and they work hard and shop Tesco Value not Sainsbury's. They said: 'what are you going to do for me? I'm not a scrounger and I'm not a millionaire.' I didn't have an answer for them."

Many losing candidates also believe that Ukip took votes from them and that this was an important factor in their defeat: "Ukip was crucial. We were told they would be a boon to us. But we lost by 2,000 and Ukip got 6,000 – it was the white working-class vote." There was a strong sense that Labour had been disproportionately hit by Ukip: "We need to speak to the people who voted Ukip . . . My gut feeling is we got a lot of the Liberal Democrat voters early on in the parliament and then we peeled off voters to the Tories and Ukip. My gut feeling is that they hurt Labour more than the Tories." Another candidate added: "Ukip took our votes – because they struck a chord with working-class Labour voters who were disillusioned."

The exit poll and the results on election night still came as a shock to many Labour people. This was confirmed by the candidates: "It was a surprise to us. We did a phenomenal amount of work, we were getting good responses. With hindsight, we could have picked up on the number of Labour voters saying they didn't know how they would vote – maybe they just didn't want to tell us." This indicates that Labour was indeed hit by a late swing to the Conservatives, probably driven by fears of an SNP-Labour coalition: "Lots of the 'don't knows' swung to the Tories, by two or three to one, including people who had swung to the Liberal Democrats previously." However, there was a feeling that better-off voters had always been reluctant to vote Labour because of their fears about the party's handling of the economy and its weak leadership: "In the more middle-class areas, I got a lot of 'don't knows' and I think they did know."

Almost all of the candidates felt that the Labour campaign was fundamentally flawed from the outset: the so-called '35 per cent strategy' meant that the party's efforts were focused on maximising turnout rather than winning over 'undecided' voters who needed reassurance about what a Labour government would mean for them: "It was a textbook campaign but it was the wrong textbook. We were mapping the political landscape rather than seeking to influence it. It was all about turnout, but we should have had textbooks about how to convert people, how to spend time with the undecideds . . . We mostly spoke to Labour people. We made 4,000 contacts a week but we didn't have a strategy that was about turning people." Labour was also out-spent and out-organised by the Conservatives: "Voters had personal letters from Cameron and three phone calls . . . A lot of that was down to money." It was not just about resources, however; the Tory campaign was sharper, better organised and more skilful in reaching out to undecided voters: "The Tories certainly did the targeted stuff better. Our mailings were all pretty much identical, they weren't very good – it was the same letter but maybe they used longer words writing to some people, it wasn't a different message to different groups. The Tories were better at micro targeting, and they got a lot more mailings to everyone."

Labour's campaign was fatally undermined by the leadership team's belief that former Liberal Democrat voters would defect to the party in droves after Nick Clegg's 'betrayal' in 2010: "I think there was complacency at the heart of the party that assumed the Lib Dems would come to Labour, and the electoral system was rigged to help Labour. Everyone should know that if you aim for 35 per cent you won't get it. The Lib Dems in our areas did not vote Labour." Former Liberal Democrat voters did not support Labour for the same fundamental reasons as voters everywhere: they did not trust Labour to manage the economy and they believed that the party had a weak, politically insubstantial leader.

This is confirmed by another candidate who said he had managed to retain the middle-class vote in his seat, but: "We didn't win the Lib Dems and that's where our strategy was completely at odds with what we should have been doing. Those Lib Dems were prepared to keep voting Tory. They are economic liberals rather than social liberals and we didn't say anything to them."

WHERE LABOUR WON

The message from our research is that the Labour candidates who won their marginal seats against the Conservatives did so by ignoring the national Labour campaign. These winning candidates wove together a sophisticated understanding of local issues with a more nuanced political appeal which highlighted their credentials and reached out to undecided voters: "I ran as an aspiration candidate. I am from a working-class background and I wanted to better myself, like my constituents – they want more prosperity, better education for their children, better healthcare and so on. Nationally, we didn't address these issues. We didn't address voters' concerns. There was a hole in our campaign and my personal story helped fill that hole . . . Our policies for those who work hard and play by the rules didn't come across in the national message."

As we have seen, Labour's campaign nationally was hampered by the fact that there was no single message and issues were often addressed in language which voters struggled to relate to: "I ran my own campaign. The trouble was that the language of the campaign wasn't the language of the voters. The leadership talked about their issues but not mine, not the agenda of my constituents . . . I had a letter saying that they liked me but they wouldn't vote for us in case

Miliband became PM!" Another successful candidate reiterated a basic truth which Labour appeared to forget for much of the 2015 campaign: "You've got to reach out to the voters; you can't win elections if you ignore the voters."

WHERE NEXT FOR LABOUR?

The candidates broadly agreed on what Labour has to do next if it is to be in a winning position by 2020: "We need a leader who is respected by members of the public, we need to stop pretending it doesn't matter if all the media is against us, we need to focus on economic competence so any policies should be based on their economic merits, and we need a simple, clear message of what Labour is today and why you should vote Labour." There was a feeling that 'one more heave' would not be enough and that the challenge for the party was more existential. Labour had to understand the ways in which British society was changing: "We need to do a lot of navel-gazing, understand what the 21st century looks like and who lives here and then think what would most deliver for those people while still retaining concern for our communities. We must never stop being the party of equality but there aren't enough of those types of people we've relied on in the last 100 years." Another candidate added: "You have to start from where the country is, and work from there. We need a fresh approach to the country's challenges. It's not about particular policies; it's about the approach to politics." As one senior party figure perceptively puts it: "Clement Attlee and Tony Blair adapted the Labour party to society and that's what we need to do: not adapt society to the Labour party". In Scotland, the message was equally stark: "We have to bring more talent into Holyrood; all the best people are in Westminster . . . We have to learn again how to be a campaigning party, rather than a status quo party. And we have to stop the in-fighting."

The political appeal that won Labour elections in the 1940s, 1960s and 1990s is unlikely to succeed in 2020. The imperative for the party is to broaden its electoral base by reaching out to a new generation of voters who want a governing prospectus combining economic competence and social justice: "We need to win in the south and rural areas. We need a credible economic policy and a leadership who can take on Cameron and Osborne. It's got to be better than the Tory leadership because our voters can find excuses not to vote and the Tory vote is solid." Too often, voters saw Labour as, "a party of the past", with too little to say to, "Self-employed, working class people – the aspirational people – [who] care about their kids' futures".

Widening Labour's electoral base means vigorously reaching out to those on middle-incomes and the struggling working and middle class: "In America they describe their classes very differently to us. The working class is everyone who gets out of bed and earns a wage and we don't have a message for those people here. We have to stand for fairness but we've got to show people that we can make their life better if you're earning the average wage. We have to say that's who we are fighting for. People don't vote in an altruistic way so we have to demonstrate how society is better when we help people who are struggling . . . We need a narrative that supports the world of business so that they can in turn support those at the bottom." Those who campaigned tirelessly for a Labour victory in 2015 are clear that the party has to make major adjustments to its political strategy and policy appeal if it is ever again to command an electoral majority in British politics.

NOTES

1. British Election Study, 'Seminar: Who Won the UK General Election, How and Why?', British Election Study, 19 May 2015, http://www.britishe-lectionstudy.com/bes-impact/seminar-who-won-the-uk-general-election-how-and-why/.
2. British Election Study (2015).
3. British Election Study (2015).

WHAT LABOUR MUST DO

The challenge for Labour in 2020 is not to devise dozens of new policies, but to confront the very real weaknesses in its positioning and political image. Labour has to regain the confidence of a sceptical electorate: having been convinced a party shares their values, voters want to be confident it has a credible governing strategy with specific, costed proposals that will make a real difference to their lives, rather than an abstract ideological vision lacking economic coherence. Labour will not secure a majority in 2020 by one more heave, dusting down a few policy ideas from the 2015 manifesto and revamping the party's logo. A more profound reconstruction of the party's appeal will be needed. To win again, Labour will have to overhaul radically its message, its strategy and its organisation. It will have to make not a narrow class or sectional appeal, but a wide, radical appeal to broad sections of the population. It will have to fight the next election on an agenda that is relevant to the 2020s not the 1990s. This chapter sets out the fifteen steps Labour must take to remake itself as a viable contender for power at the next election.

First, Labour must be a party of power: unless you are in government, you can do nothing to help the less fortunate in society. As in the 1980s, the party in 2015 stacked up big majorities in many 'core' Labour areas of England, but it can do little for the most disadvantaged communities unless the party can also win seats in the Midlands and southern England. This obvious point was forgotten for much of the 1980s and in the 1950s as well. Labour must never forget that a better society can only be achieved by winning and retaining power.

In *Politics as a Vocation*, Max Weber distinguished between "the ethic of ultimate ends" and "the ethic of responsibility".[1] Those who pursue the goal of ultimate ends are interested only in what they consider to be morally right: they are unwilling to contemplate consensus, pragmatism or compromise but simply want to retain their moral and ideological purity. Those who follow the ethic of responsibility, on the other hand, are prepared to face up to hard choices and to accept the need for priorities, securing political power in order to introduce social reforms that meaningfully improve the lives of working people. Labour needs to stop treating power and principles as irreconcilable, but instead pursue both. That also means ensuring that the plight of the least fortunate in society resonates with those who are well-off and lead more comfortable lives.

Second, Labour has to build electoral support across social classes. The party has to be a pluralistic grouping necessarily seeking support from every section of the community, rather than a narrowly tribal party pursuing the dominance of one class over another. Labour needs to purge itself of the sectarian mindset that still prevails in certain sections of the party. Labour has to appeal to a much wider group of voters than in 2015 if it is to win and retain power, including the many who voted Conservative last time. Britain is becoming a predominantly middle-class society: more people work in middle-class occupations, and more people identify themselves as 'middle class'. Labour forgets this fact at its peril.

Third, Labour has to make an argument to the country based on a marriage of social justice and individual aspiration. It has to protect the vulnerable by making further progress in tackling poverty, while also being the party of upward mobility and the equal opportunity society. Labour's mission must be to break down barriers that hold people back, encouraging every individual to fulfil their true potential, highlighting the areas where the Conservatives are falling short on their promises while challenging established institutions and 'closed' professions that entrench privilege.

Fourth, Labour will only win if it is perceived to be an economically competent party. The Labour party was blamed by the voters for the financial crash in 2008 and has yet to regain their confidence seven years on. Labour has to demonstrate that it is committed to fiscal discipline and does not see more public spending as the solution to every problem.

Prior to the 1997 election, Tony Blair and Gordon Brown announced they would stick to the spending limits of the previous Conservative government, setting out new fiscal rules ensuring "prudence with a purpose". Next time, Labour will need to propose robust fiscal objectives such as a balanced budget annually on current spending, overseen by an independent institution such as a beefed up Office for Budgetary Responsibility (OBR) reporting directly to parliament. This new prudence is necessary to reassure the public that the British economy can weather global shocks while leaving scope for much-needed capital investment. The OBR should have an additional role in monitoring the effectiveness and productivity of government spending on public services.

The absence of a coherent growth strategy on the part of the previous coalition government created a potential opportunity for Labour in 2015, which it duly squandered. Labour failed to outline a new growth model to promote future jobs in the British economy, to develop new industries and to advance new technologies. Where markets are not working effectively, there is a role for government intervention, including sustained public investment in key strategic infrastructure, alongside the upgrading of skills and innovation. The state has a role to play in rebalancing the economy, moving Britain away from its reliance on low-wage, low-skill, low-productivity sectors: a modern industrial strategy ought to focus on regional specialisation and lead technologies such as carbon capture and storage. The burgeoning green economy has the potential to be a vital source of new growth and jobs. The digital economy will create further opportunities for employment and wealth creation. This can only be achieved by creating effective partnerships between the public and private sectors rather than condemning businesspeople and entrepreneurs as 'predators'. Labour has to show that it is committed to the production of wealth, as well as its redistribution.

Fifth, Labour must always be a party that aims to achieve rising living standards. In 2015, Labour highlighted the extent to which real wages and the standard of living had declined in Britain since the early 2000s. The evidence indicates that the earnings of those on middle incomes – between £20–30,000 per annum – were being increasingly compressed. If the so-called 'squeezed middle' is defined as those clustered around the median of the income distribution, those voters have visibly failed to gain from rising prosperity.[2] Labour should have had a compelling critique in 2015 of an economy which was failing those on middle incomes and the middle class, but by focusing on zero-hours employment contracts and the living wage alone it struggled to appeal to the relatively affluent workers – the skilled working-class and white-collar occupational groups – who did not believe that the party had much to offer aspiring, upwardly mobile voters. Enabling the majority to share in the benefits of rising affluence means diffusing wealth and asset ownership as widely as possible through the promotion of employee share ownership and profit-sharing schemes, as envisaged by the John Lewis Partnership model where every employee receives an annual dividend payment in addition to their salary. The government can set an example: rather than selling 100 per cent of the shares in the Royal Bank of Scotland to private investors, one-third should have gone to a trust managed on behalf of customers, and a further third to the employees of the bank.[3] This would have spread the benefits of dividend payments far more widely than conventional investors in the stock market. Labour has to rethink the structures of ownership in the British economy.

It is likely that Labour will fight the 2020 election against the backdrop of a recovery in real wages and, in comparison to the last decade, a mood of rising affluence and prosperity. The party will need to show how Labour can support people's desire for increased personal consumption, as well as stronger public services. In fact, high income taxes on ordinary wage-earners were never part of Labour's original programme: in 1945, only 12 million families in Britain had paid income tax even after a substantial expansion of the tax system during the war; by the end of the 1990s, the figure had reached 26.9 million.[4] Social democracy has to abandon its obsession with achieving the laudable objectives of resilient public finances, well-funded public services and fairer distribution through income tax alone. This means keeping the burden of income tax on middle-income earners as low as possible, while supporting low-paid families in work through the living wage, better targeted efforts to improve skills and earning power, alongside extra measures such as help with childcare. To justify levying income tax, Labour will need to demonstrate that standards in state-funded health and education are as high as anything available in the private sector.

In 2015, Labour's case for fairer taxes focused on its commitment to address tax avoidance and tax evasion, while restoring the 50p income tax rate for those on the highest incomes. While Miliband's argument that those with the broadest shoulders should contribute the most to dealing with the financial crisis was a reasonable one, Labour is in danger of boxing itself into a corner on tax by focusing too narrowly on the distribution of income. Labour's goal should be to allow people to keep as much of their hard-won earnings as possible, but to tax the proceeds of unearned wealth, capital and property. The Mirrlees Review of Taxation undertaken by the Institute for Fiscal Studies proposed a shift from direct to indirect taxes, replacing regressive taxes such as stamp duty and council tax with new levies on property. An annual property tax on the most expensive homes would enable a Labour government to give additional tax relief to low- and middle-income tax payers.

Reforming tax allowances and moving more people out of the tax system altogether is politically appealing, but the most efficient way to raise family incomes and reduce child poverty beyond the national minimum wage is still through targeted tax credits. Labour needs to review the entire system of tax credits, however, reemphasising that they are primarily about supporting those in work, particularly families and are therefore 'earned', while stripping out wasteful administrative complexity and bureaucracy.

Sixth, Labour has to make public services more responsive and efficient. Labour learned from being in government in the 1990s and 2000s that it is not enough to pour more money into the public sector. Bizarrely, after 2010 when money was tighter, the party decided an emphasis on reform was no longer important. But, the state has to become even more cost-effective today: public services have to be genuinely responsive to peoples' needs if the consensus for universal, taxpayer funding is to be sustained in an era of greater choice, individualism and rising expectations. It must be Labour that identifies new integrated models for organising public services to achieve 'more for less', capturing the productivity gains that have revolutionised other sectors of the economy. A Labour government should strive to cut costs dramatically, making public services more effective while never conceding the mantle of public sector efficiency to the right.

If Labour wants to reassure voters that public money is being spent wisely, it ought to consider the option of 'hypothecation', directing taxes towards specific areas of spending, such as paying for health and social care. The Treasury has traditionally been hostile to 'earmarking' taxes since it reduces the flexibility of governments to direct resources to where they are most needed, although in the 2015 budget, the chancellor levied an apprenticeship levy to pay for training and a rise in vehicle excise duty to fund road repairs. The aim of hypothecation is to make citizens feel better 'connected' to the taxes they pay. There needs to be much greater transparency, with citizens receiving information about how money is spent and what impact it is having. Every household in Britain could receive a 'citizens' statement' which explains how the tax system works and how public spending is being allocated.

Seventh, Labour has to build a 21st century welfare state that offers genuine social security for all. Rather than a narrow debate about welfare cuts, Labour must develop innovative social policies, 'a new Beveridge' that restores confidence in the contributory principles of the social security system. After 2010, Labour flirted with the idea of reviving the contributory approach, but small-c conservatism kicked in; by the 2015 election, Labour's message on welfare amounted to little more than abolishing the bedroom tax. The welfare system we have today was designed in the 1940s for a world of heavy industry and predominantly male breadwinners facing risks such as unemployment, sickness and lack of access to decent housing. Life expectancy was markedly lower, as were people's expectations of a decent standard of life. Today, many of the traditional risks are still with us, but people increasingly face 'new' risks: lack of skills, family instability, the difficulty of reconciling work and family life, and a much longer old age. In the meantime, public attitudes to the welfare state have become more hostile and punitive: there is a feeling that some are taking out more than they are putting into the system.

Labour as the party of Beveridge must recognise that nothing short of a complete root and branch overhaul of the social security system is required. Old rules and assumptions need to be revisited. Rebuilding contributory social insurance has many advantages, but those who advocate returning to the contributory principle of the postwar era need to explain how those groups outside the formal labour market, such as carers and those who are only able to find temporary employment, will be covered by such a system. On pensions, Labour has been outmanoeuvred by government reforms which liberalise the annuities market, giving more power to individuals to manage their own money: while such changes transfer significant risk to individuals, the centre left is on the wrong side of the argument if it tries to tell people what is good for them.

A further theme concerns the extent to which younger people and families are being systematically disadvantaged by government policy. The pension 'triple lock' ensures a guaranteed 2.5 per cent increase in the state pension each year; at the same time, education spending is being cut with fewer resources going to post-16 tertiary education; tax credits and in-work benefits that support families with children are being hit; and the government's goal of a budget surplus serves to protect today's older taxpayers.[5] Indeed, the arbitrary pursuit of a surplus in government spending merely transfer's debt to private households: the OBR estimates that household borrowing will be 170 per cent of national income by 2020, above its level immediately prior to the financial crisis. Meanwhile, cutting spending on public services weakens Britain's long-term competitiveness and growth potential, just as maintaining low interest rates encourages investors to flock into risky assets in an already inflated property bubble, further preventing young people from getting their foot on the housing ladder.[6]

Eighth, Labour has to confront openly the debate about immigration in Britain. Labour should certainly not compete with Ukip in voicing hostility to immigration. What the party says must be honest and credible: if Britain wants to remain a member of the EU, or even enjoy the free trade benefits that Norway has as a member of the European Economic Area, it cannot renege on freedom of movement although it is, of course, essential to tackle abuses such as people-trafficking and so-called 'benefit tourism'. Imposing tighter controls on migration from outside the EU would prevent the NHS from attracting skilled doctors and nurses, while undermining student recruitment to British universities. Immigration can be good for Britain economically and culturally. Immigrants bring new skills and will be needed even more in the future, as the population continues to age.

However, there must be effective oversight of the system and a crackdown on illegal immigration; hard-pressed communities must be compensated with more resources to ease the pressures on public services in local areas; and immigrant newcomers should be expected to uphold certain values and obligations. People already living in Britain want to feel listened to, rather than having their views dismissed by an out of touch political establishment. Voters complain they are depicted as 'racist' by politicians if they complain about immigration (hardly surprising given what happened to Gillian Duffy in Rochdale) – so it is important that Labour in particular listens hard to what they are saying.

Resentment towards immigrants is fuelled by lack of jobs, overcrowded infrastructure and, in particular, the crisis in the housing system. The acute shortage of affordable housing markedly increases social resentment and is a major barrier to families fulfilling their aspirations. Many young people are compelled to rent for longer, particularly in London and the south-east. As well as building more homes, Labour should focus on tougher regulation of the private rented sector, curbing excessive rent rises and improving security of tenure. Labour also needs an agenda to extend home ownership through introducing more sustainable forms of finance and credit, while radically expanding the availability of land to increase the supply of affordable housing.

Ninth, Labour has to continue to be the party of local government. By winning power locally and running local councils effectively, particularly in parts of the country where the party does not currently have MPs, Labour can demonstrate its governing competence. Osborne has temporarily stolen the mantle of localism and devolution from Labour with his proposal for a 'northern powerhouse', an idea that emerged under the Blair and Brown governments when powers were handed back to local communities after decades of centralisation. The answer for Labour is not to turn its back on devolution, but to demonstrate that it is more determined than the Conservatives to give back genuine powers to local people, including greater fiscal autonomy. Moreover, Labour should advance a vigorous regional economic strategy that promotes growth and employment in the most disadvantaged areas of Britain. The party needs a particular focus on former industrial areas which it has rather taken for granted since the 1980s. It is time to stop blaming Thatcherism and to develop an active industrial policy that promotes new jobs and dynamic industries with higher wages. In any case, voters have increasingly hazy memories of the Thatcher years: younger and even middle-aged voters in 2020 will have little recollection of the Thatcher governments after 1979.

Great Britain, and more particularly England, is one of the most centralised countries in the industrialised world, eroding faith in democracy and politics which is particularly damaging to the centre-left cause. Instead of allowing power to be hoarded at the centre, Labour has to decentralise power as widely as possible. Citizens in England want to feel as well represented as they do in Scotland, Wales and Northern Ireland; and they want to know that Labour has an affinity with the places, communities and cultures that populate England. The party should not be afraid to recognise and speak up for the political identity of the English, directly addressing the resentments flowing from a devolution settlement that gives Welsh and Scottish voters a stronger voice. The Tories' plan for English votes for English laws on its own increases the centralisation of power in Westminster and Whitehall, as do proposals for an English parliament. A new settlement for English local government is needed alongside a constitutional convention that considers the case for a federal Britain.

This new settlement has to include far greater fiscal freedoms, giving local councils additional borrowing powers to set business rates and to establish local business levies to fund specific projects such as infrastructure improvements. There should be fewer central targets overseeing local public services: as far as possible accountability should be located locally to the citizen. Every city and combined authority in England should have its own directly elected mayor with powers similar to the big cities in the United States, providing voters agree locally in a referendum. In 2012, referenda to approve the introduction of mayors in many English cities were defeated, although that was as much a reflection of the coalition government's overly cautious approach to the devolution of power. Devolution, localism and empowerment are about more than allowing citizens to elect a mayor every five years: citizens need to have additional rights including rights of initiative such as owning community assets; recalling representatives where public services locally are failing; and decentralising further powers to the neighbourhood level. Labour needs to resolve its confused and half-hearted position on the devolution question.

Tenth, Labour needs a strategy to win back Scotland. This will be a difficult task, it will take time and it will have to start from the bottom up. Scotland deserves a full and complete analysis of its own, as indeed does Wales, where having achieved its lowest share of the vote since 1918 at the 2010 election, Labour managed only a 0.6 per cent improvement in 2015. Great Britain is a more electorally variegated country than ever: as Vernon Bogdanor has pointed out, this is the first election in modern political history where a different party has won in each of the four constituent nations of the UK.[7] In Scotland, there were specific factors which help to explain the seismic loss of Labour voters to the SNP. As one activist explained: "We had a long-term structural issue. There were decaying parties, constituencies where we were suffering from 'safe-seat-itis', we took them for granted and then we were hit by a tsunami. We didn't challenge the SNP in power properly; we waited for them to implode. We can't outflank the SNP as a nationalist party, we did the right thing in remaining a unionist party, but this provided the SNP with a handy attack in the election."

It seems clear that the factors underlying Labour's defenestration in Scotland go beyond the 2014 independence referendum. The referendum certainly sowed the seeds: according to John Curtice of the University of Strathclyde, 35 per cent of those who voted Labour in 2010 voted to leave the UK in 2014. Astonishingly, 50 per cent of those who voted to remain in the UK in 2014 voted SNP in 2015. As Curtice acknowledges, Labour has been on the back-foot in Scottish politics for more than a decade since it failed to develop any convincing vision or national project for Scotland after the Scottish parliament had been created in 1999. Margaret Thatcher left office in 1990. Twenty-five years later, Labour was still attempting to anchor its electoral appeal in not being the Tories. The weakness of this strategy was exposed as early as the 2007 Scottish parliamentary elections, when the SNP began to make major gains. Increasingly, votes no longer wanted a 'partnership' between London and Edinburgh, but a party that would stand up resolutely for Scottish interests; they were attracted by the SNP's vision of social equality which Labour appeared to have abandoned in the 1990s, as Curtice has shown. According to the 2015 British Election Study, SNP voters were, on average, more supportive of redistribution than those who opted to stick with Labour, although there is little evidence that Scottish voters are fundamentally to the left of those across the rest of the UK: the recent British Social Attitudes survey reveals that while 43.8 per cent of Scots favoured higher taxes and higher spending, for example, the figure in England was 36.4 per cent.[8] The authors of the study conclude that Scotland is depicted as more leftwing and social democratic than it actually is. In addition, the SNP has been pioneering new models of partici-patory democracy and deliberative engagement in Scotland which reinforce Labour's image as the last bastion of a failed political cul-ture (although the SNP have, in fact, further centralised control over Scottish public spending).

Curtice concludes that we may now be witnessing the end of British politics: the political system is fragmenting and the consti-tutional futures of Scotland, England, Wales, as well as of Northern Ireland, are fundamentally in question. Ironically, the scenario most likely to stem the rise in SNP support is granting full fiscal auton-omy to Scotland: under the Barnett formula Scottish public spending is 20–25 per cent higher than Scottish tax receipts. The SNP has endorsed a set of policies – notably free university tuition, free social care and free public transport for the over-65s – which are both fiscally regressive and which largely fail to address the future com-petitiveness challenges facing Scotland. For example, to fund free higher education tuition, the SNP government has been forced to cut budgets for further education, vocational training and Scotland's apprenticeship programme. This is hardly the way to develop the skilled future workforce that Scotland needs, nor is it very consis-tent with the principle of social justice as resources are ever-more skewed towards middle-class households. Labour in Scotland must become a campaigning party, capable of taking the argument to the SNP, building up strength and confidence at Holyrood, and striving to win back seats at Westminster. The crunch in SNP support may not come for some time, but Labour must begin by setting out a compelling social democratic alternative that judiciously combines economic efficiency with social justice for Scotland.

Eleventh, as a matter of priority Labour has to revitalise and modernise the party in both its traditional strongholds and in the south and the Midlands. We should build up community organisations as a way of strengthening local parties. Labour has to champion a new form of community politics where local issues are at the forefront of campaigning. There ought to be a special role for the 2015 parliamentary candidates, many of whom fought impressive individual campaigns at the election. The party should develop a new generation of candidates and councillors, particularly in the south where Labour is chronically under-represented. Above all, Labour still has a reputational problem: even the name of the party is off-putting to large sections of the British population, redolent as it of heavy industry and the cloth cap. 'Labour' gives the impression that the party stands for an interest group rather than a vision of society in a world where people see themselves as consumers and citizens, not only as workers and producers. The former steelworkers' union renamed itself as Community and is flourishing. There is little to be gained by Labour in formally changing its name, but the party ought to learn lessons from the trade unions that have successfully updated their image and appeal.

Labour will need to symbolise its conversion to the new politics by opening up the party to wider society, electing its leader and deputy leader through an open primary in which all Labour supporters can participate. All future parliamentary selection contests should be conducted through open primaries to ensure greater participation by party supporters; though special care must be taken to guard against entryism by those who do not support Labour's aims and values. The policymaking process underpinning the party's next manifesto should be opened up to the public with opportunities through face-to-face meetings and digital technology to join the debate. Labour party conference ought to become a two-day event with fewer formalities and more opportunities for direct political engagement: Labour must project itself as a dynamic social movement rather than a narrow interest group. Young people in particular are often interested and engaged in their communities, but put off by bureaucratic Labour party meetings: there needs to be stronger encouragement of local activity and more community involvement, harnessing the potential of social media. Youth mayors and youth parliaments have also proved effective in involving young people in the political process, and Labour ought to encourage more of them.

Labour's values are enshrined in the 'new' clause IV of the party constitution adopted by the party in 1995 proclaiming that "we achieve more together than we achieve alone." Now 20 years old, the new clause IV was a revision that ought to have taken place in the 1950s, rather than the 1990s. Today, the party needs a new and up to date statement of values fit for the modern world. The new clause IV produced by Blair and John Prescott quite rightly sought to jettison the party's obsolete commitment to wholesale nationalisation, and it would be a dangerously retrograde step to return to Sidney Webb's 1918 formula. The clause IV we need today has to be a modern affirmation of social democratic values as a marriage of social justice and individual freedom augmented by a commitment to internationalism and environmental sustainability. Rather than leaping straight into a debate about its 2020 manifesto, Labour needs a wide-ranging review of its broader ambitions for society involving people outside the party, not least through dialogue with liberals, greens and other progressive forces. It needs to reach out to new sources of energy in civil society. Labour has to recreate the broad-based movement for constitutional and political renewal it forged in the early 1990s.

In relation to Scottish Labour, the party should have autonomy from London, but the English, Welsh and Scottish Labour parties must develop a shared social democratic vision for the whole of

Britain. There has to be a distinctive English Labour party, too, and Labour must fight the 2020 election with an English manifesto. It is vital that Labour projects itself as a party capable of speaking up for English political interests given the rising tide of English nationalism.

Twelfth, Labour has to renew its relationship with the trade unions. Whatever its origins, Labour must be – and be seen to be – much more than a trade union party. It must be a broad, one nation party, concerned with seeking national solutions for national problems. Although the party should respect trade union views and oppose attempts to curtail the right to collective organisation, it can never allow itself to be dominated by an interest group, however influential and powerful it may be. For their part, the trade unions cannot afford to allow themselves to be portrayed as primarily political organisations. The relationship between a Labour government and the trade unions should be mainly a consultative one.

The party therefore needs to continue to modernise the link between its political and industrial wings. The Collins review proposals introduced by Miliband have led to the abolition of the electoral college, and the introduction of a system of one member, one vote for electing the party leader and deputy leader. Following the 2015 leadership election, Labour should review how well the new system is working given widespread concerns about its credibility. Labour must ensure a fairer balance of representation on the National Executive Committee (NEC) of the party where, currently, the trade unions have two-thirds of the seats. Local councillors in particular should have a much stronger voice on the NEC. At party conference, trade unions still have 50 per cent of the votes: that needs to be reformed so that ordinary members and registered supporters have the major say in the party's policymaking process.

Thirteenth, Labour has to advance a new politics in Britain, where necessary seeking an accord with the Liberal Democrats. This is not a matter of an electoral pact or tactical agreement with the Liberal Democrats (or any other party) which magically produces a centre-left government. It remains the case, however, that the

Conservatives were able to win in 2015 against a divided centre left. As John Maynard Keynes predicted in 1925, the 20th century was overwhelmingly a conservative century because Labour and the Liberals were divided into separate parties. Social democrats and liberals ought to be able to work together on matters of common interest: how to keep Britain at the heart of the EU; how to update Britain's constitution to create a vibrant federal polity; and how to advance social justice while protecting the civil liberties of the British people.

Labour should offer a warm welcome to disillusioned Liberal Democrats who are now seeking a radical home. And if circumstances change, Labour should not rule out a progressive alliance with the Liberal Democrats, driven by a joint agenda of civic and political renewal. There should be dialogue with other political parties on issues of shared concern, including the Green party. When faith in politics declines to such low levels, constitutional reform can never be a panacea for apathy and disengagement: politicians urgently need to reconnect with voters. Britain's political culture will not change, however, until there is wider reform of our anachronistic institutions. That should include the full democratisation of the second chamber, stronger parliamentary scrutiny of decision-making in Whitehall and Westminster, radical devolution, and further opportunities for citizen engagement in the governing process.

Fourteenth, Labour has to be an internationalist, not an isolationist party. Labour is pro-European rather than Eurosceptic. The party has long believed that Britain must play a leading role in Europe, and that the EU is crucial for jobs, growth and living standards throughout Britain. Growing threats on the borders of Europe from the Middle East to the Ukraine ought to be addressed through a common European security strategy. Labour is a patriotic party but that is not inconsistent with keeping the UK at the heart of Europe: Britain's interests are best served if it pursues a pro-European approach working with our allies to ensure we meet the security and economic challenges of the future. It was the Labour foreign secretary Ernest Bevin who played a leading role in establishing Nato in 1949, and the party must reaffirm its continuing support. And under a Labour government, Britain should retain an independent nuclear deterrent.

Finally, Labour has to have effective political leadership. Choosing the right leader is crucial for the party's success. A successful leader of a centre-left party must have the capacity to combine empathy with strength. Empathy means keeping the party together while reaching out beyond Labour to speak to, and for, the whole of the electorate, understanding their hopes and fears. Strength means being courageous, bold and decisive, as well as good in a crisis, recognising that Labour is a party which voters believe has its heart in the right place, but has too often lacked the courage to take tough decisions and see through change in difficult times. Last but not least, Labour's leader needs to combine a firm commitment to the party's values with a sensible pragmatism about their means of implementation. Labour has to accept the reality of Britain as it is today and look to the future not the past.

NOTES

1. This distinction is elaborated by Anthony Crosland, see Crosland (1960).

2. Lansley, S. (2010), *Life in the Middle: The Untold Story of Britain's Average Earners,* London: Trade Union Congress, https://www.tuc.org.uk/sites/default/files/documents/lifeinthemiddle.pdf.

3. Goodway, N. 'Here's a Radical Sell-off Scheme that Could Speed RBS Back to Popularity', *The Evening Standard,* 16 June 2015, http://www.standard.co.uk/business/markets/nick-goodway-a-radical-selloff-scheme-that-could-speed-rbs-back-to-popularity-10323690.html.

4. Clark, T. and Dilnot, A. (2002), *Long-Term Trends in British Taxation and Spending,* London: Institute for Fiscal Studies, http://www.ifs.org.uk/bns/bn25.pdf.

5. Inman, P. 'Five Ways George Osborne Will Fail the Next Generation', *The Guardian,* 15 June 2015. http://www.theguardian.com/business/2015/jun/15/five-ways-george-osborne-fail-next-generation-analysis

6. Inman (2015).

7. In England, the Conservatives won the most votes; in Wales, Labour; in Scotland, the SNP; and in Northern Ireland, the Democratic Unionist party.

8. Brooks, L. 'Three Things the Latest British Social Attitudes Survey Tells Us About Scotland', *The Guardian,* 26 March 2015, http://www.the-guardian.com/uk-news/scotland-blog/2015/mar/26/three-things-the-latest-british-social-attitudes-survey-tells-us-about-scotland.

CONCLUSION
Labour's Hard Road to Power

If Labour is to recast itself as an attractive national party representing Britain's mainstream majority, it has to rediscover its radical roots, not merely defend the institutions and gains of the past. In recent years, despite its high-flown rhetoric, the party has risked becoming a force of conservatism and inertia, rather than of radical change. Ed Miliband wanted to take Britain back to the world of the 1970s, not forward to the 2020s. Labour's mission is not to consolidate the gains of the Attlee era or the Blair-Brown era: it is to change British society to ensure that wealth, power and opportunity lie in the hands of the whole national community, rather than a narrow and privileged elite. The party can be proud of what it has achieved but it needs to stop looking backwards and instead offer a persuasive vision of where Britain needs to be in the future, recognising all of the dangers but also the opportunities of the modern age.

The 2015 election results demonstrated that if voters in Britain want to support a conservative party, then they will vote for the real thing. There is an appetite for a political party that faces up to, and seeks to address, the major long-term challenges facing the UK, but it can only be done on the basis of establishing economic credibility and political trust. The voters of middle England are ready to hear a message from Labour which is open about the hard choices and trade-offs ahead, instead of promising all things to all people while engaging in the futile politics of protest. At the same time, under a new leader Labour has to articulate a story of hope: the party's argument must be that with a Labour government by 2030, Britain can be among the richest, the most socially compassionate *and* the most environmentally sustainable countries in the world. Voters do not have to choose between future prosperity, the future of the planet and a fairer, stronger, more equal society.